MAX AXIOM AND THE SOCIETY OF SUPER SCIENTISTS

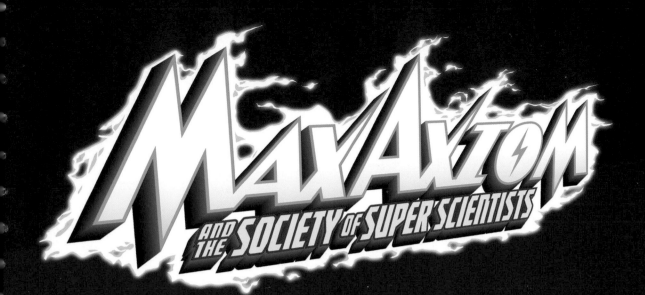

CLIMATE CHANGE ON THE BRINK

BY CAROL KIM
ILLUSTRATED BY KATHARINE DOESCHER

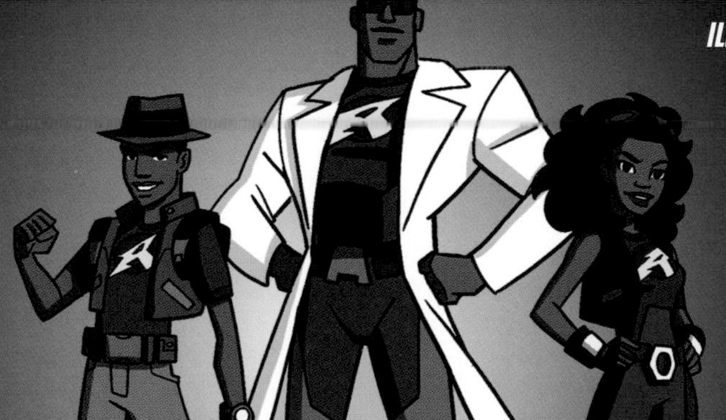

CAPSTONE PRESS
a capstone imprint

Published by Capstone Press, an imprint of Capstone.
1710 Roe Crest Drive
North Mankato, Minnesota 56003
capstonepub.com

Library of Congress Cataloging-in-Publication Data
Names: Kim, Carol, author.
Title: Climate change on the brink : a Max Axiom super scientist
    adventure / Carol Kim.
Description: North Mankato, Minnesota : Capstone Press, [2022] | Series:
    Max Axiom and the society of super scientists | Includes bibliographical
    references and index. | Audience: Ages 8-11 | Audience: Grades 4-6
Summary: "Earth's climate is changing. Heat waves and droughts are more
    common and more severe. Powerful hurricanes cause widespread
    damage. And polar regions are warming fast, causing even more
    problems around the world. Why is this happening? In this nonfiction
    graphic novel, Max Axiom and the Society of Super Scientists go on an
    exciting, fact-filled adventure that will help young readers learn about
    the causes and effects of climate change and learn ways that they can
    make a difference"-- Provided by publisher.
Identifiers: LCCN 2021020830 (print) | LCCN 2021020831 (ebook) |
    ISBN 9781663959171 (hardcover) | ISBN 9781666322521 (paperback) |
    ISBN 9781666322538 (pdf) | ISBN 9781666322552 (kindle edition)
Subjects: LCSH: Climatic changes--Juvenile literature. | Climatic changes--
    Comic books, strips, etc. | Global warming--Juvenile literature.
Classification: LCC QC903.15 .K535 2022 (print) | LCC QC903.15 (ebook) |
    DDC 551.6--dc23
LC record available at https://lccn.loc.gov/2021020830
LC ebook record available at https://lccn.loc.gov/2021020831

Editorial Credits
Editor: Aaron Sautter; Designer: Brann Garvey; Media Researcher: Morgan
Walters; Production Specialist: Laura Manthe

All internet sites appearing in back matter were available and accurate
when this book was sent to press.

Printed and bound in the United States of America. PO4608

TABLE OF CONTENTS

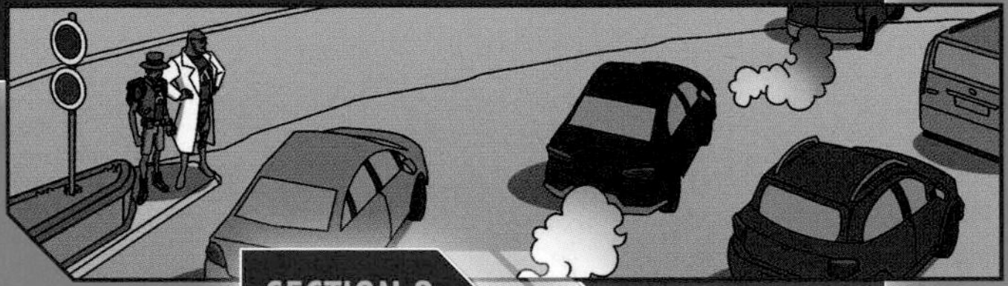

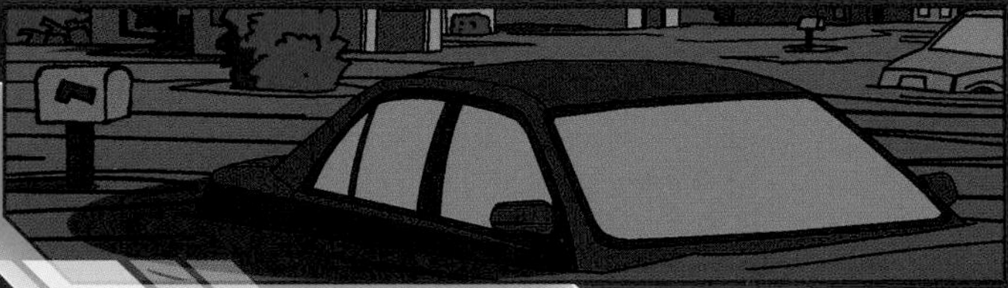

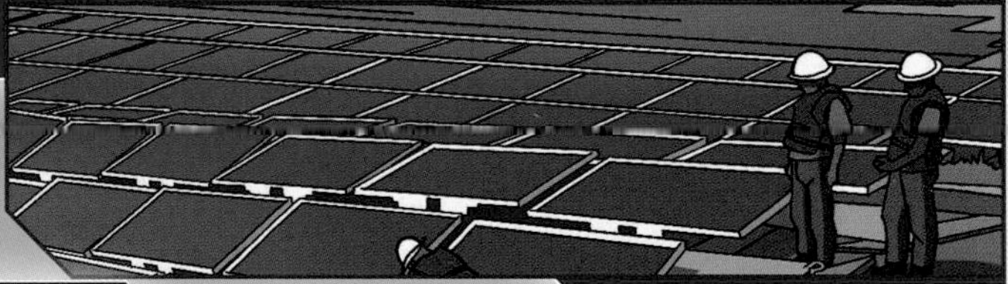

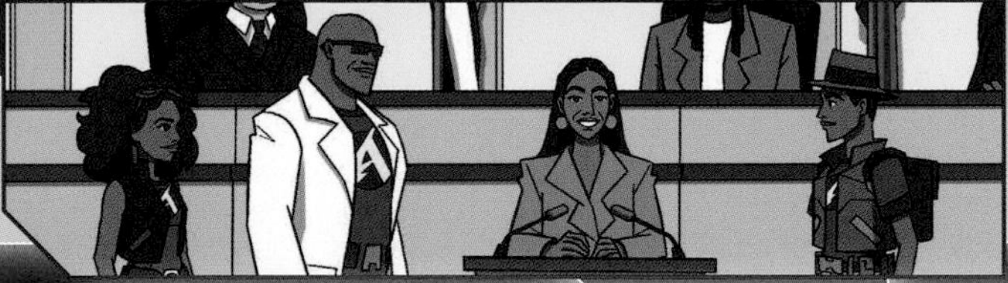

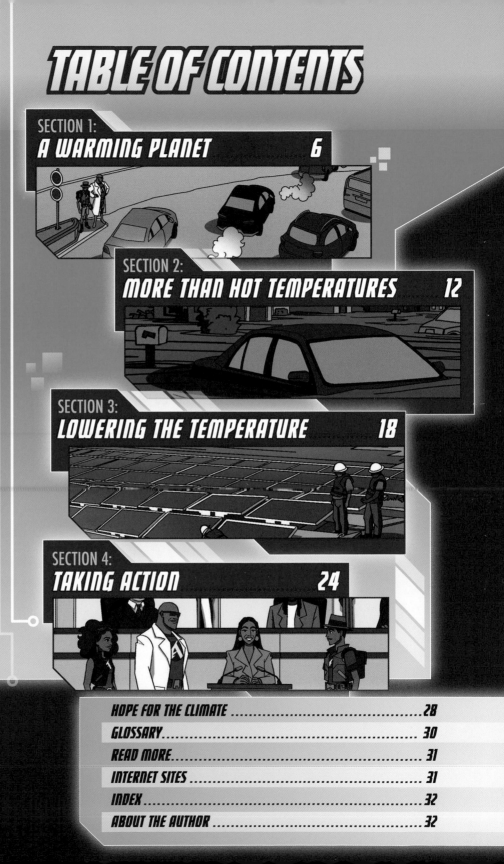

THE SOCIETY OF SUPER SCIENTISTS

MAX AXIOM

After years of study, Max Axiom, the world's first Super Scientist, knew the mysteries of the universe were too vast for one person alone to uncover. So Max created the Society of Super Scientists! Using their superpowers and super-smarts, this talented group investigates today's most urgent scientific and environmental issues and learns about actions everyone can take to solve them.

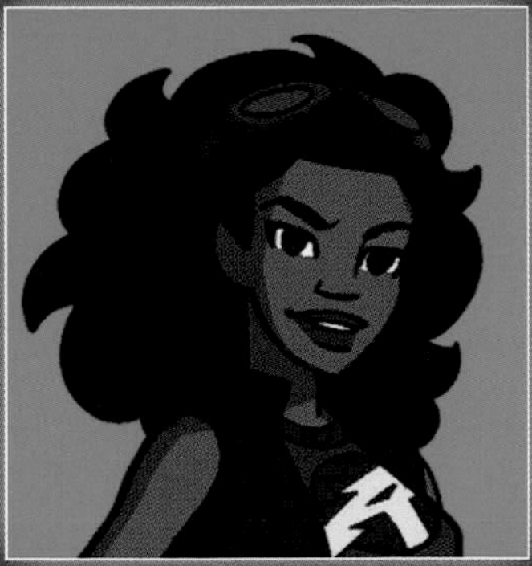

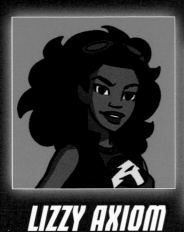

LIZZY AXIOM

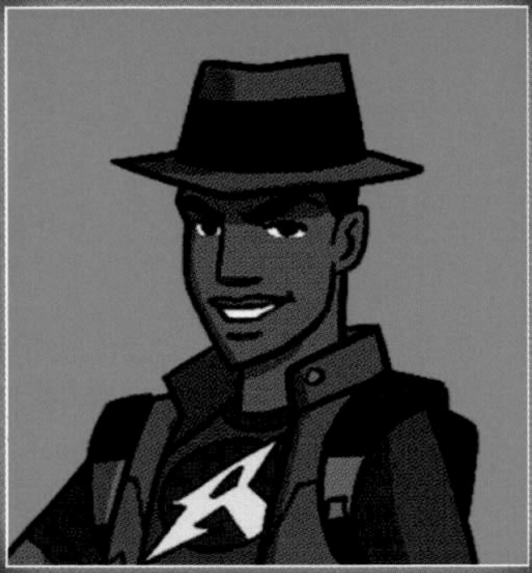

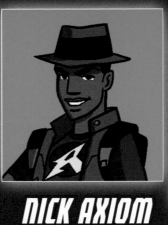

NICK AXIOM

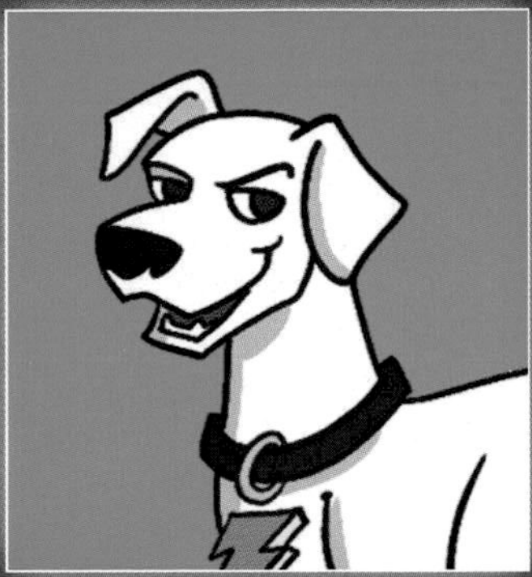

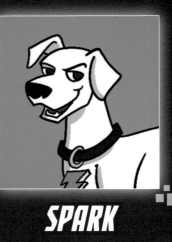

SPARK

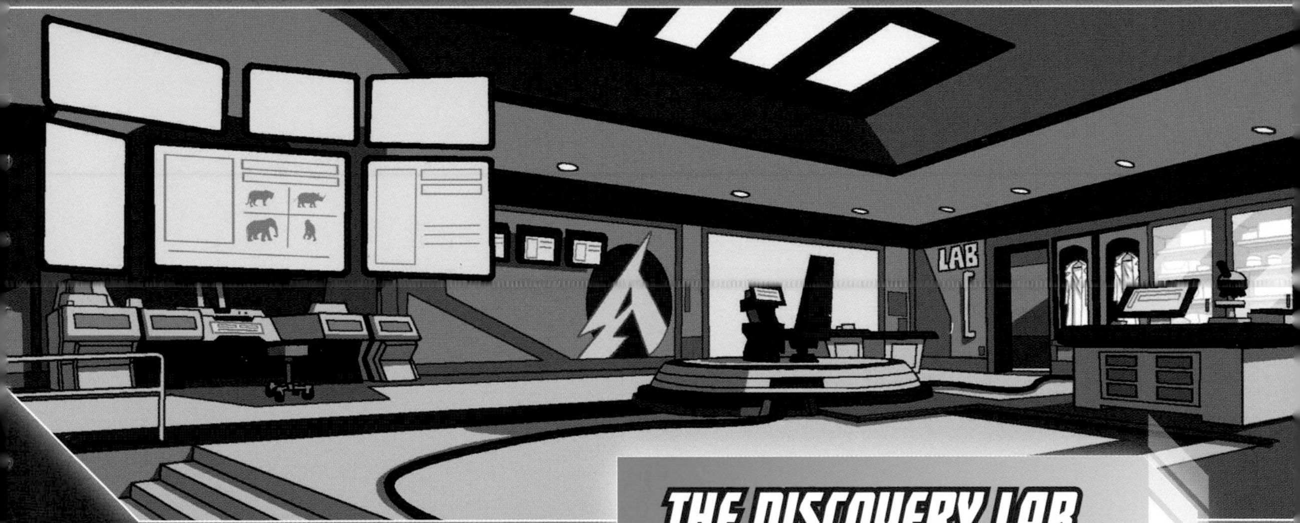
LAB

THE DISCOVERY LAB

Home of the Society of Super Scientists, this state-of-the-art lab houses advanced tools for cutting-edge research and radical scientific innovation. More importantly, it is a space for Super Scientists to collaborate and share knowledge as they work together to tackle any challenge.

SECTION 1: A WARMING PLANET

At the Discovery Lab, the Super Scientists are packing donated toys and clothes to send to kids affected by wildfires in California. But they have a lot of questions about the fires.

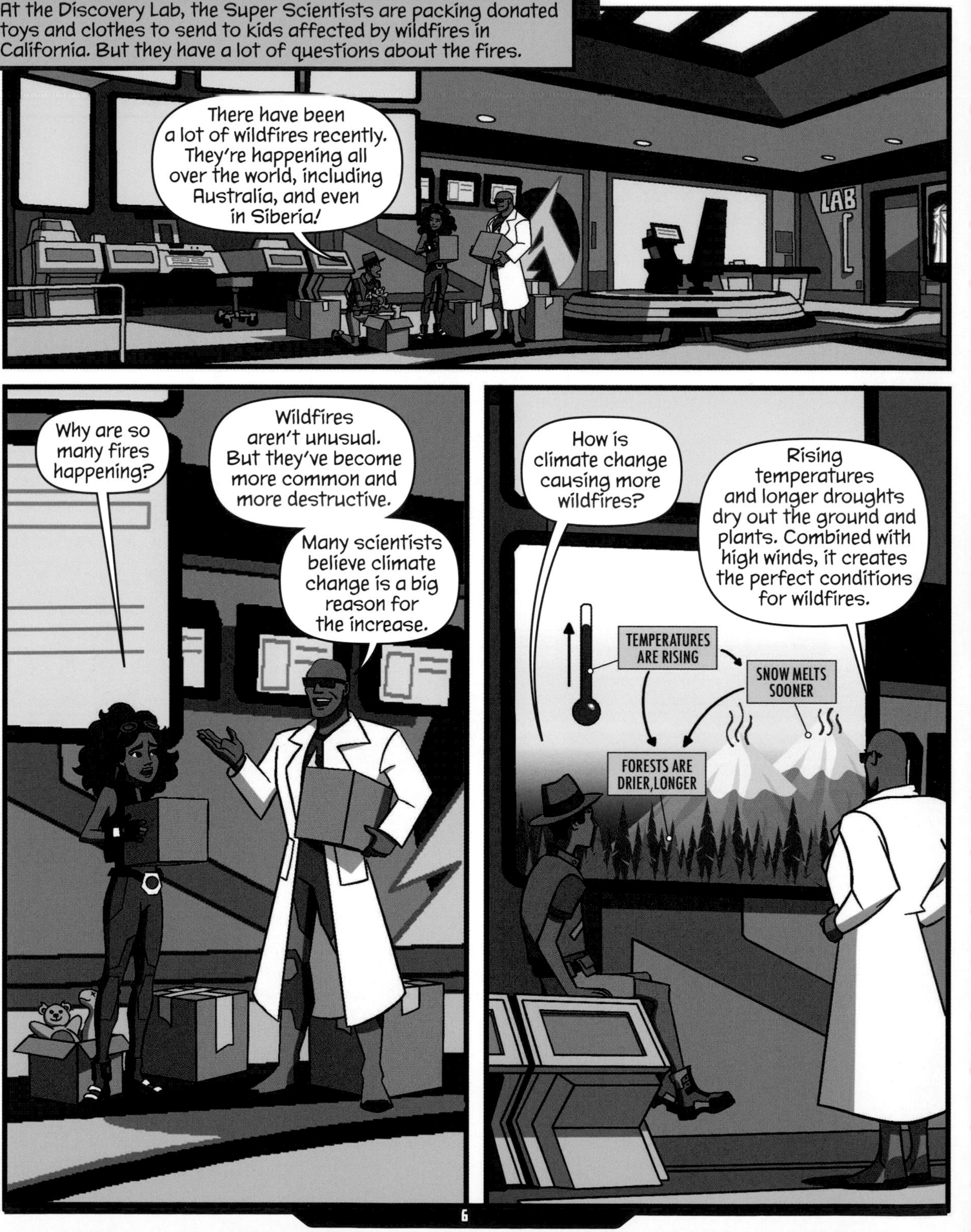

There have been a lot of wildfires recently. They're happening all over the world, including Australia, and even in Siberia!
LAB
Why are so many fires happening?
Wildfires aren't unusual. But they've become more common and more destructive.
Many scientists believe climate change is a big reason for the increase.
How is climate change causing more wildfires?
Rising temperatures and longer droughts dry out the ground and plants. Combined with high winds, it creates the perfect conditions for wildfires.
TEMPERATURES ARE RISING
SNOW MELTS SOONER
FORESTS ARE DRIER, LONGER

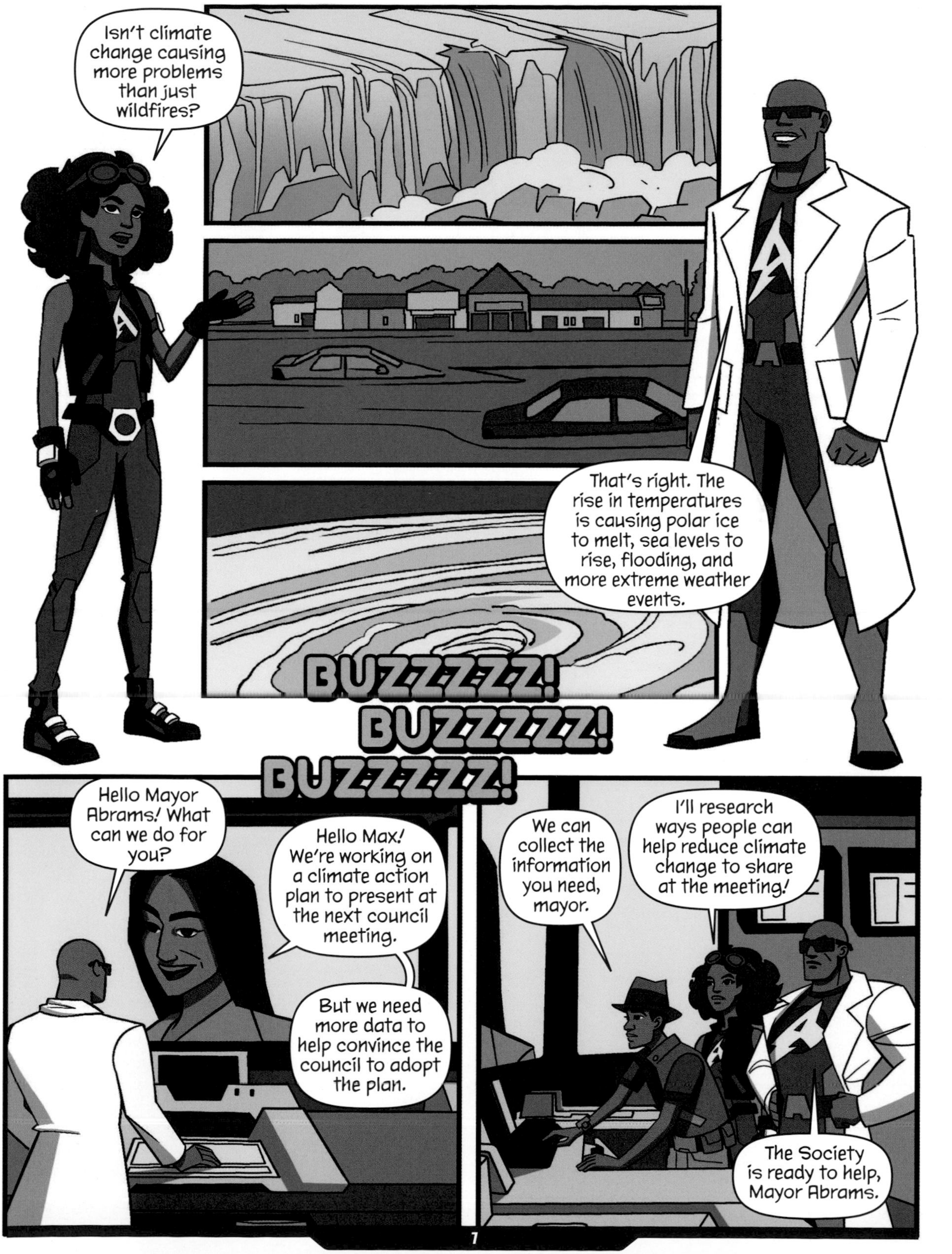
Isn't climate change causing more problems than just wildfires?
That's right. The rise in temperatures is causing polar ice to melt, sea levels to rise, flooding, and more extreme weather events.
BUZZZZZ! BUZZZZZ! BUZZZZZ!
Hello Mayor Abrams! What can we do for you?
Hello Max! We're working on a climate action plan to present at the next council meeting.
But we need more data to help convince the council to adopt the plan.
We can collect the information you need, mayor.
I'll research ways people can help reduce climate change to share at the meeting!
The Society is ready to help, Mayor Abrams.

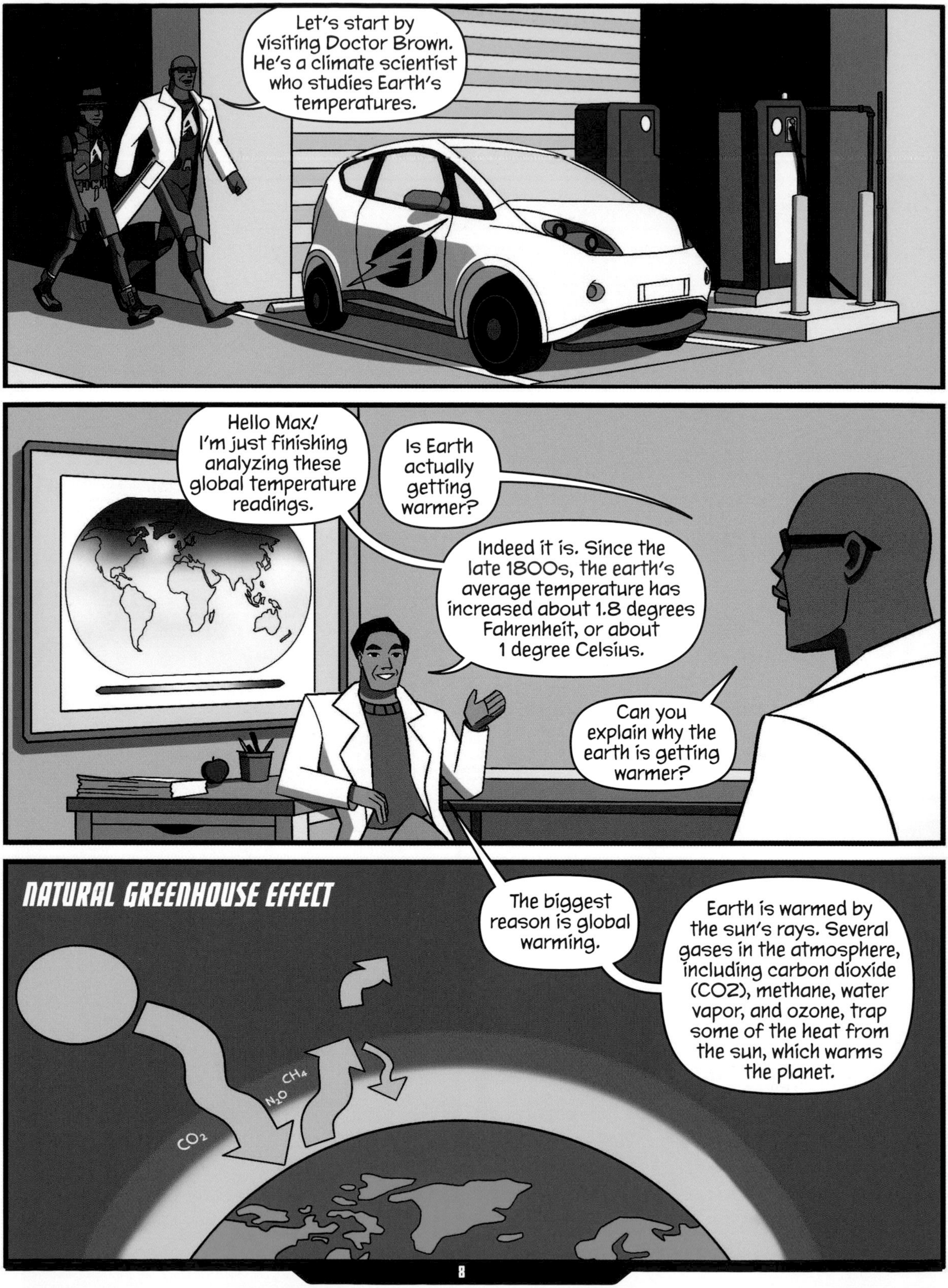

Let's start by visiting Doctor Brown. He's a climate scientist who studies Earth's temperatures.
Hello Max! I'm just finishing analyzing these global temperature readings.
Is Earth actually getting warmer?
Indeed it is. Since the late 1800s, the earth's average temperature has increased about 1.8 degrees Fahrenheit, or about 1 degree Celsius.
Can you explain why the earth is getting warmer?
NATURAL GREENHOUSE EFFECT
The biggest reason is global warming.
Earth is warmed by the sun's rays. Several gases in the atmosphere, including carbon dioxide (CO2), methane, water vapor, and ozone, trap some of the heat from the sun, which warms the planet.
CH₄
N₂O
CO₂

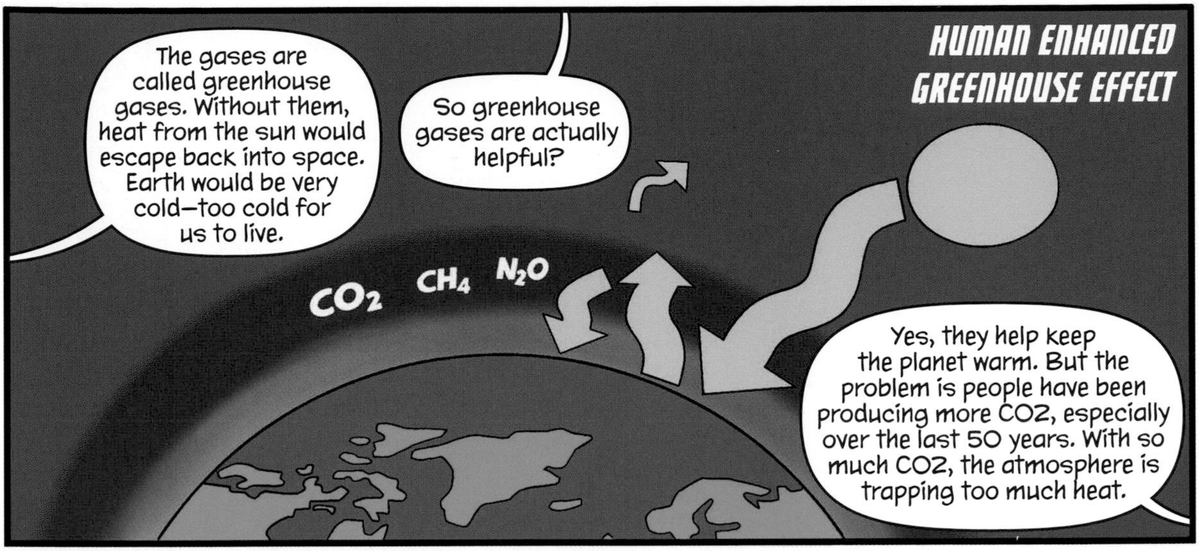
HUMAN ENHANCED GREENHOUSE EFFECT
The gases are called greenhouse gases. Without them, heat from the sun would escape back into space. Earth would be very cold—too cold for us to live.
So greenhouse gases are actually helpful?
CO2 CH4 N2O
Yes, they help keep the planet warm. But the problem is people have been producing more CO2, especially over the last 50 years. With so much CO2, the atmosphere is trapping too much heat.

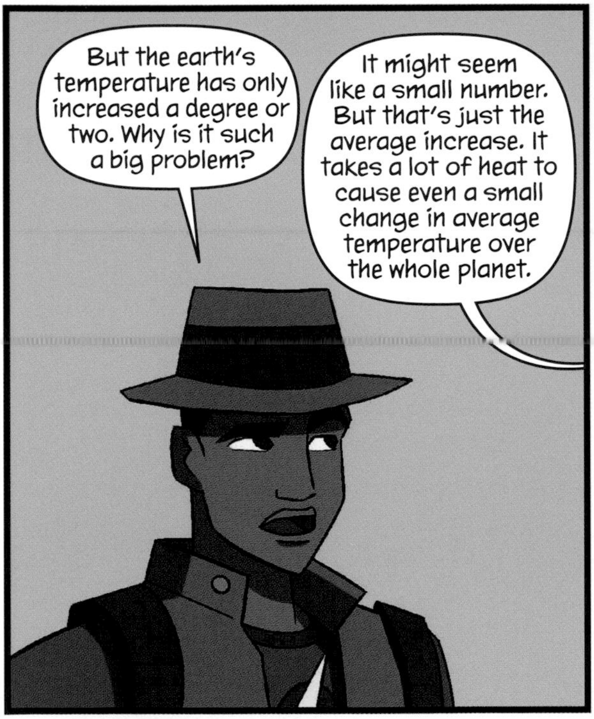
But the earth's temperature has only increased a degree or two. Why is it such a big problem?
It might seem like a small number. But that's just the average increase. It takes a lot of heat to cause even a small change in average temperature over the whole planet.

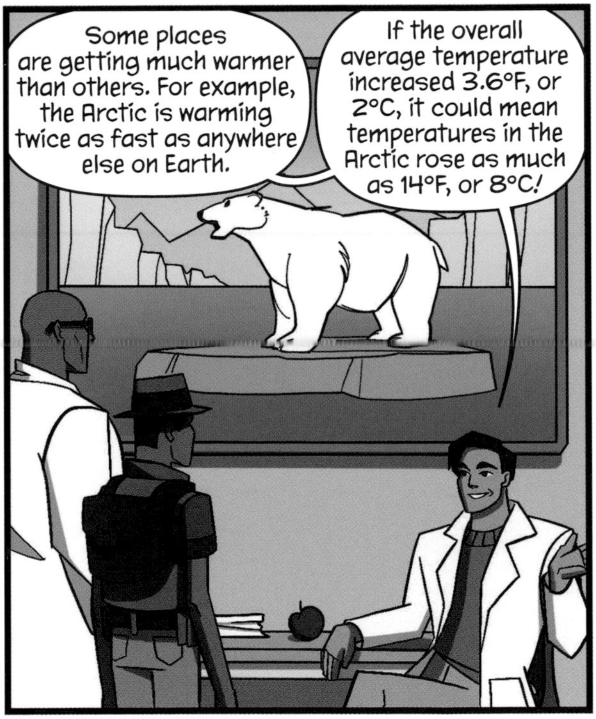
Some places are getting much warmer than others. For example, the Arctic is warming twice as fast as anywhere else on Earth.
If the overall average temperature increased 3.6°F, or 2°C, it could mean temperatures in the Arctic rose as much as 14°F, or 8°C!

WILD FIRES

Some of the worst wildfires have happened in a surprising place: the Arctic. Record high temperatures added to the problem. The Russian town of Verkhoyansk was the first place above the Arctic Circle to ever get above 100°F (38°C) in June 2020.

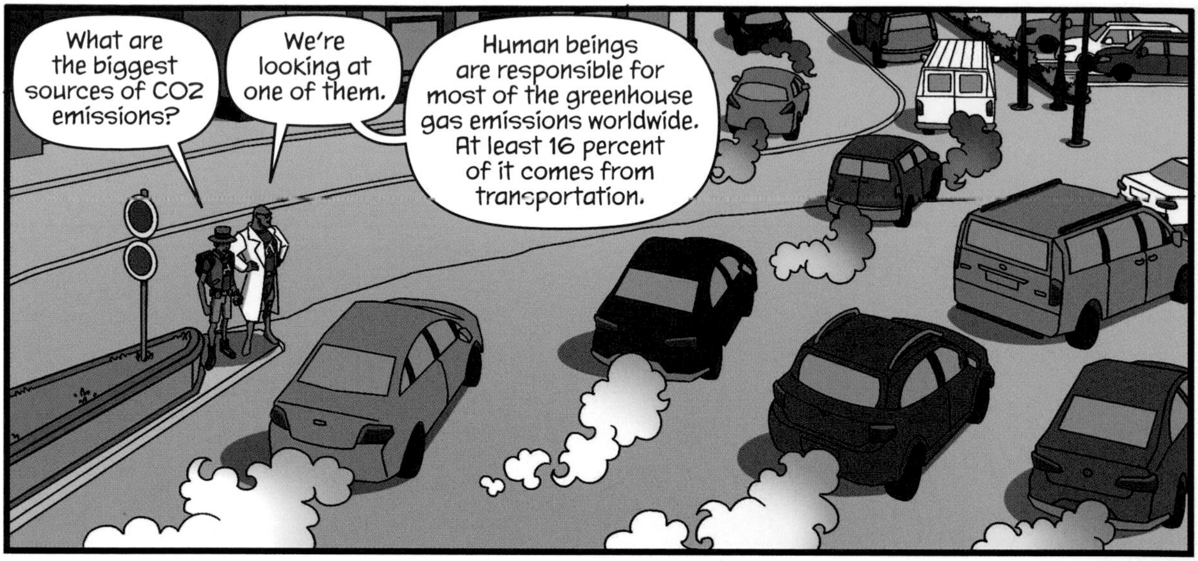
What are the biggest sources of CO2 emissions?
We're looking at one of them.
Human beings are responsible for most of the greenhouse gas emissions worldwide. At least 16 percent of it comes from transportation.

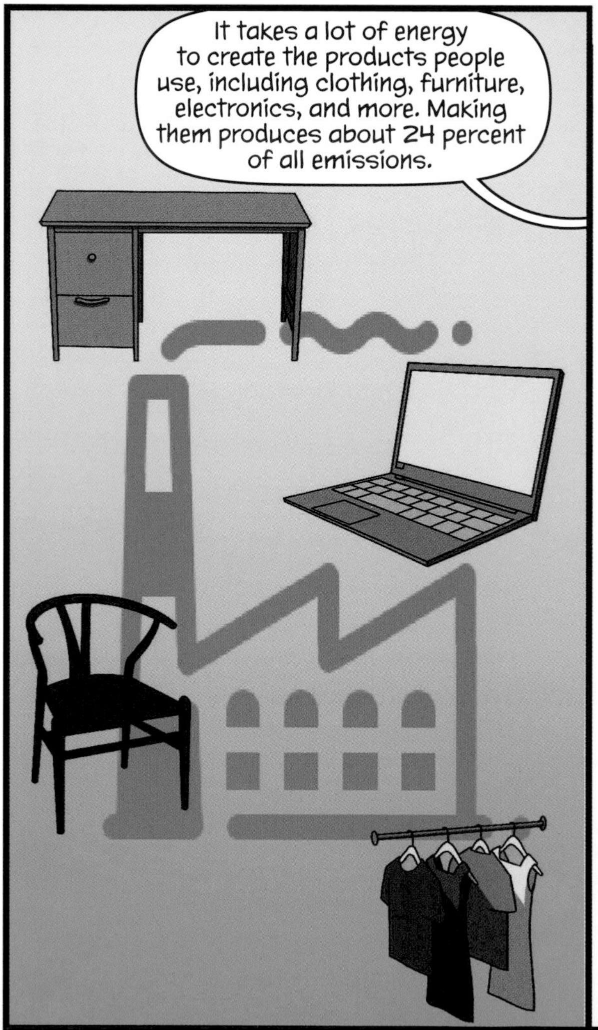
It takes a lot of energy to create the products people use, including clothing, furniture, electronics, and more. Making them produces about 24 percent of all emissions.

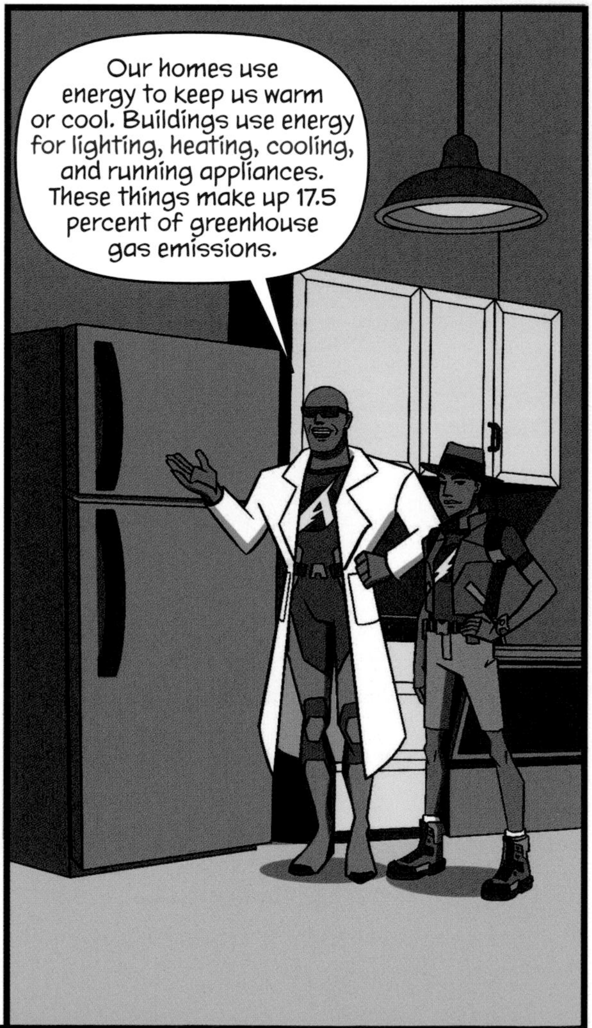
Our homes use energy to keep us warm or cool. Buildings use energy for lighting, heating, cooling, and running appliances. These things make up 17.5 percent of greenhouse gas emissions.

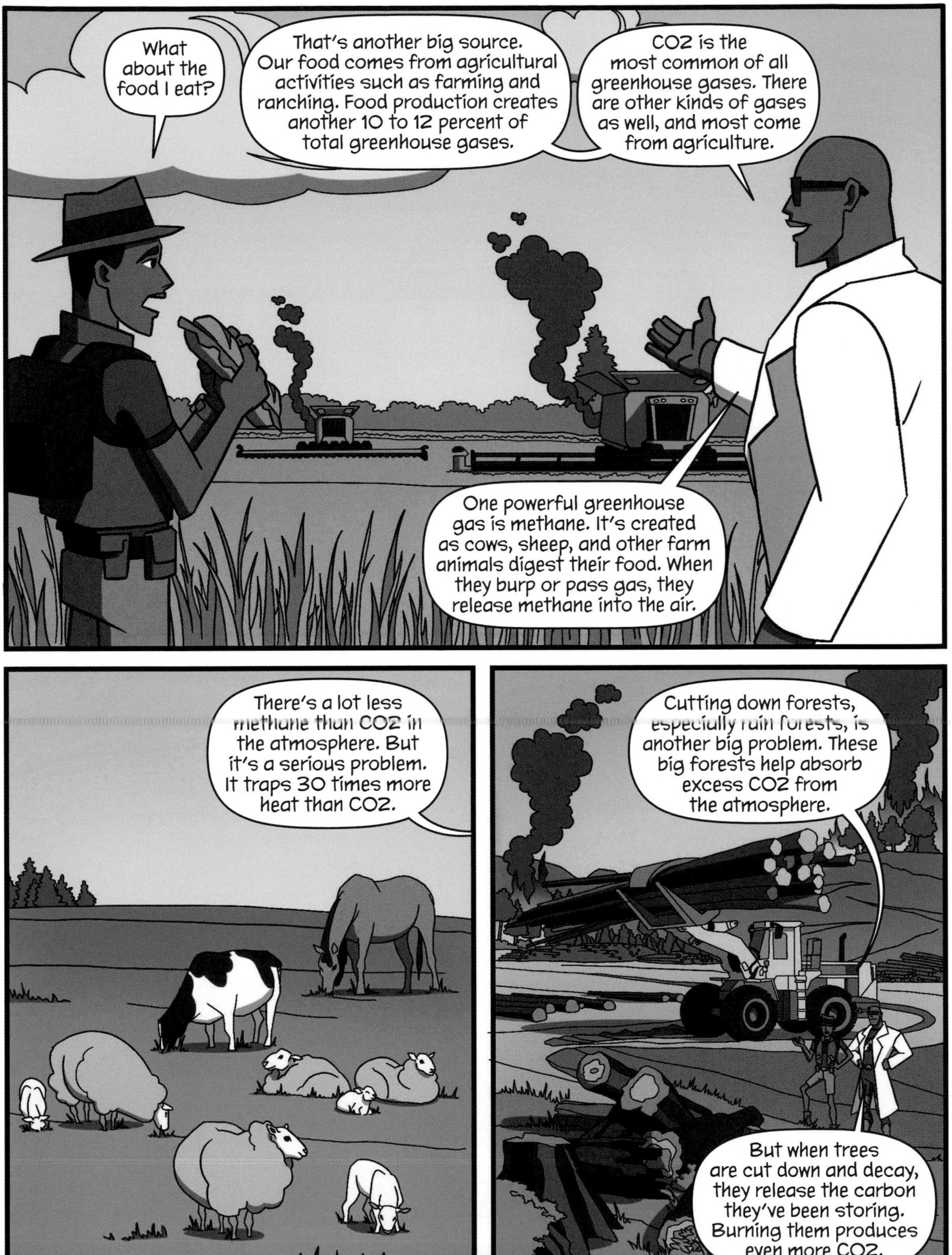
What about the food I eat?
That's another big source. Our food comes from agricultural activities such as farming and ranching. Food production creates another 10 to 12 percent of total greenhouse gases.
CO2 is the most common of all greenhouse gases. There are other kinds of gases as well, and most come from agriculture.
One powerful greenhouse gas is methane. It's created as cows, sheep, and other farm animals digest their food. When they burp or pass gas, they release methane into the air.
There's a lot less methane than CO2 in the atmosphere. But it's a serious problem. It traps 30 times more heat than CO2.
Cutting down forests, especially rain forests, is another big problem. These big forests help absorb excess CO2 from the atmosphere.
But when trees are cut down and decay, they release the carbon they've been storing. Burning them produces even more CO2.

SECTION 2: MORE THAN HOT TEMPERATURES

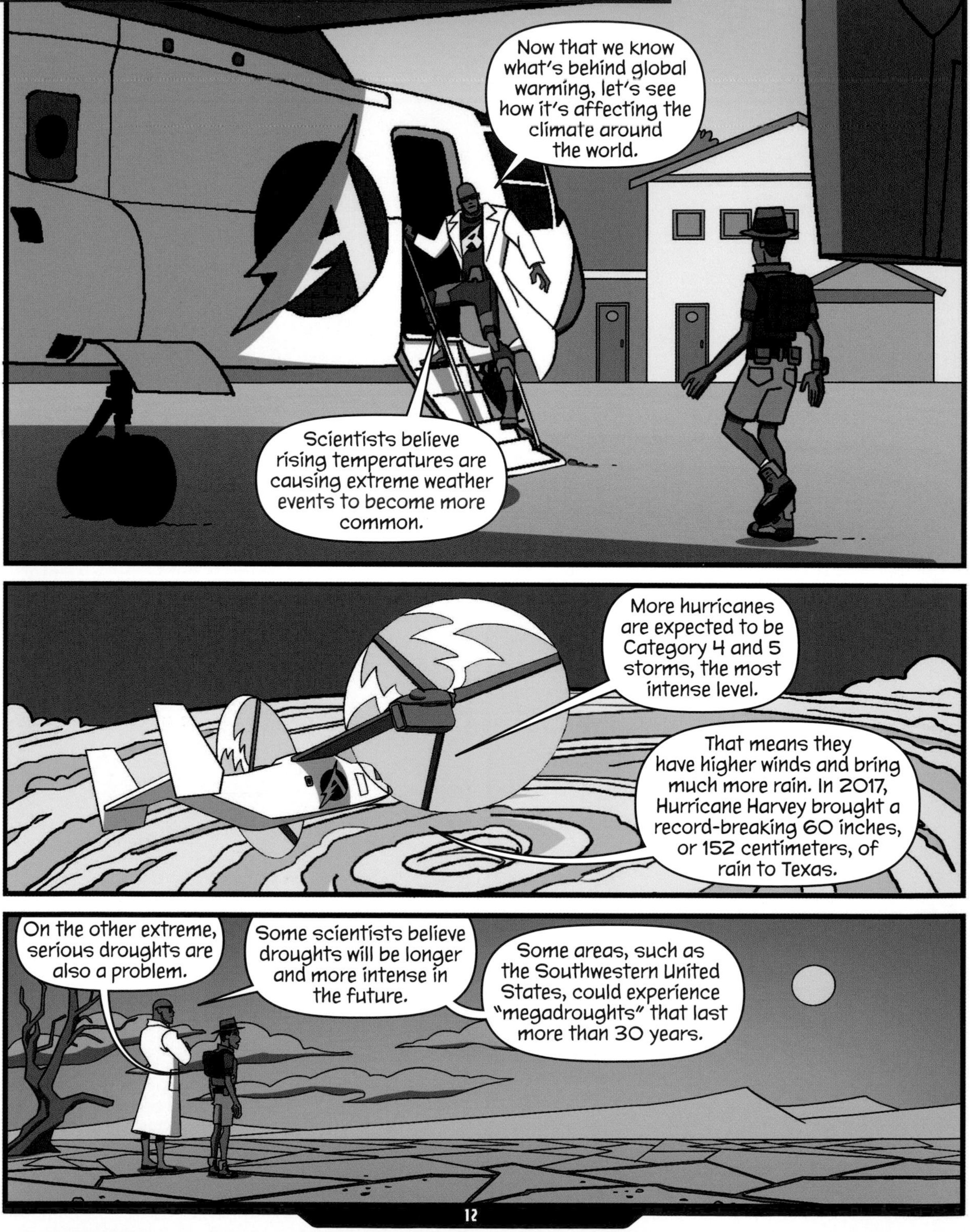

Now that we know what's behind global warming, let's see how it's affecting the climate around the world.
Scientists believe rising temperatures are causing extreme weather events to become more common.
More hurricanes are expected to be Category 4 and 5 storms, the most intense level.
That means they have higher winds and bring much more rain. In 2017, Hurricane Harvey brought a record-breaking 60 inches, or 152 centimeters, of rain to Texas.
On the other extreme, serious droughts are also a problem.
Some scientists believe droughts will be longer and more intense in the future.
Some areas, such as the Southwestern United States, could experience "megadroughts" that last more than 30 years.

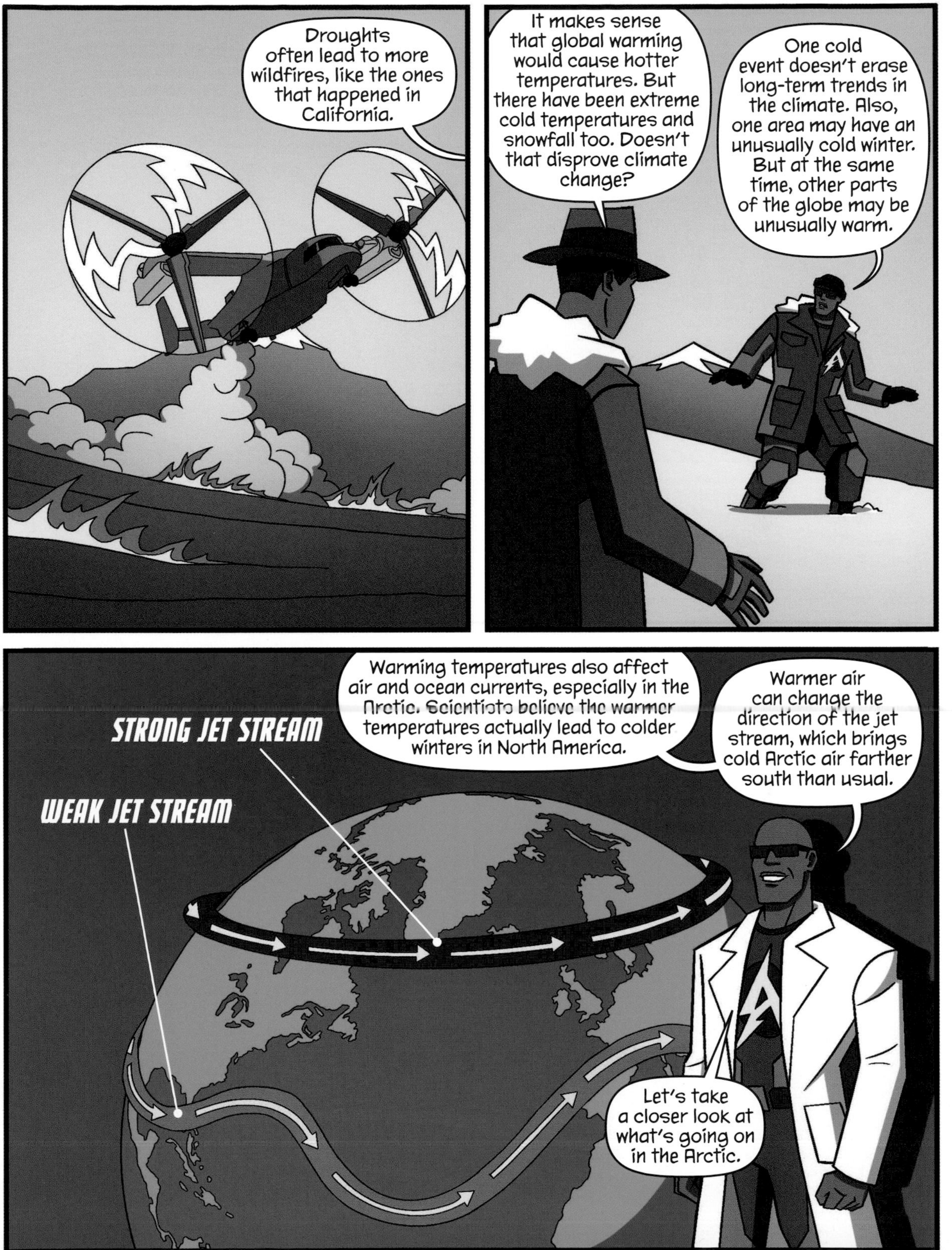
Droughts often lead to more wildfires, like the ones that happened in California.
It makes sense that global warming would cause hotter temperatures. But there have been extreme cold temperatures and snowfall too. Doesn't that disprove climate change?
One cold event doesn't erase long-term trends in the climate. Also, one area may have an unusually cold winter. But at the same time, other parts of the globe may be unusually warm.
Warming temperatures also affect air and ocean currents, especially in the Arctic. Scientists believe the warmer temperatures actually lead to colder winters in North America.
Warmer air can change the direction of the jet stream, which brings cold Arctic air farther south than usual.
STRONG JET STREAM
WEAK JET STREAM
Let's take a closer look at what's going on in the Arctic.

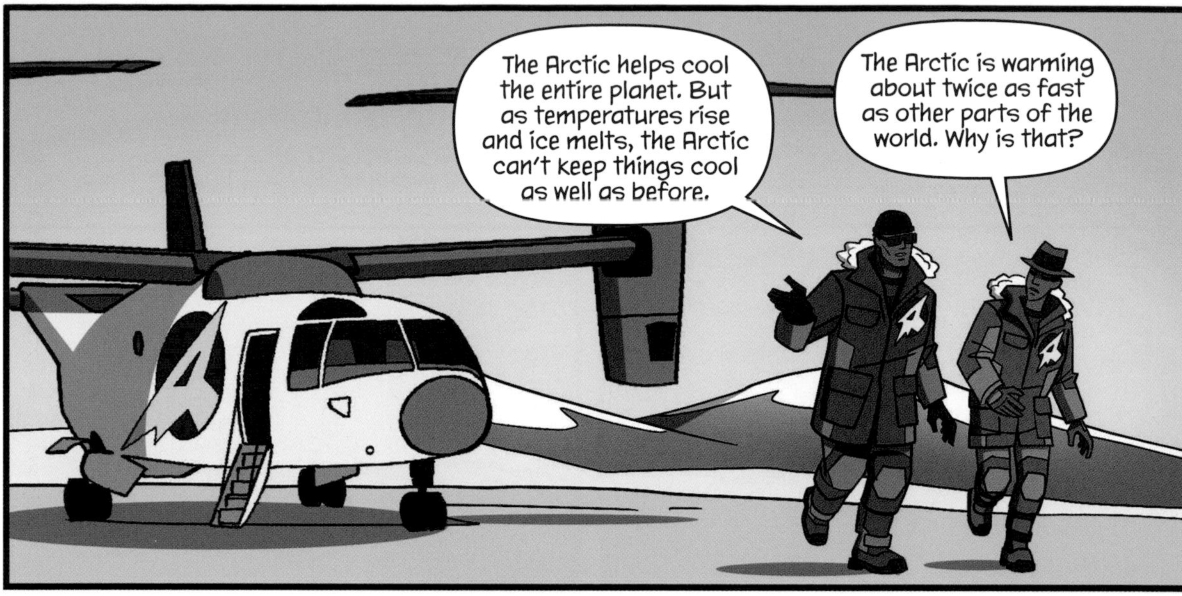
The Arctic helps cool the entire planet. But as temperatures rise and ice melts, the Arctic can't keep things cool as well as before.
The Arctic is warming about twice as fast as other parts of the world. Why is that?

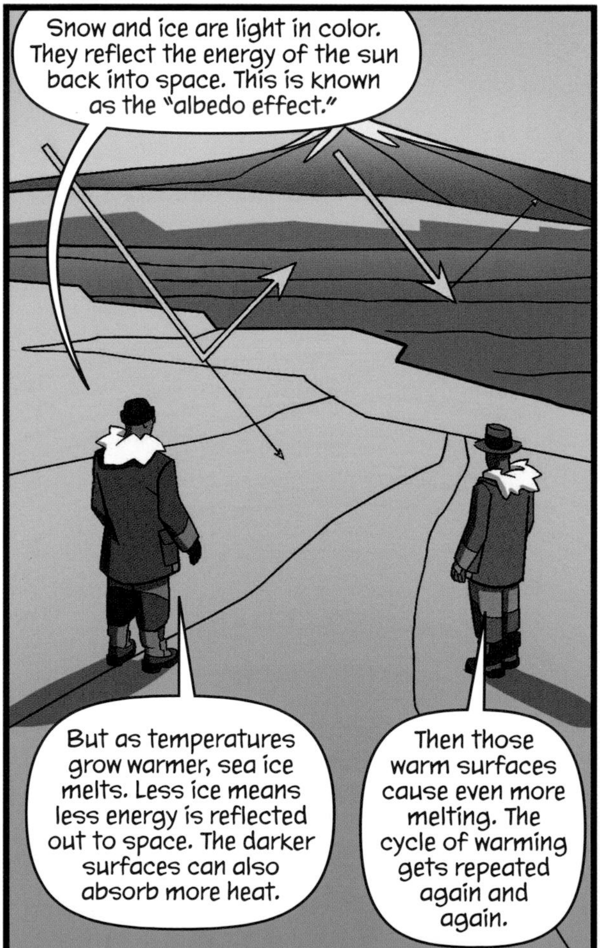
Snow and ice are light in color. They reflect the energy of the sun back into space. This is known as the "albedo effect."
But as temperatures grow warmer, sea ice melts. Less ice means less energy is reflected out to space. The darker surfaces can also absorb more heat.
Then those warm surfaces cause even more melting. The cycle of warming gets repeated again and again.

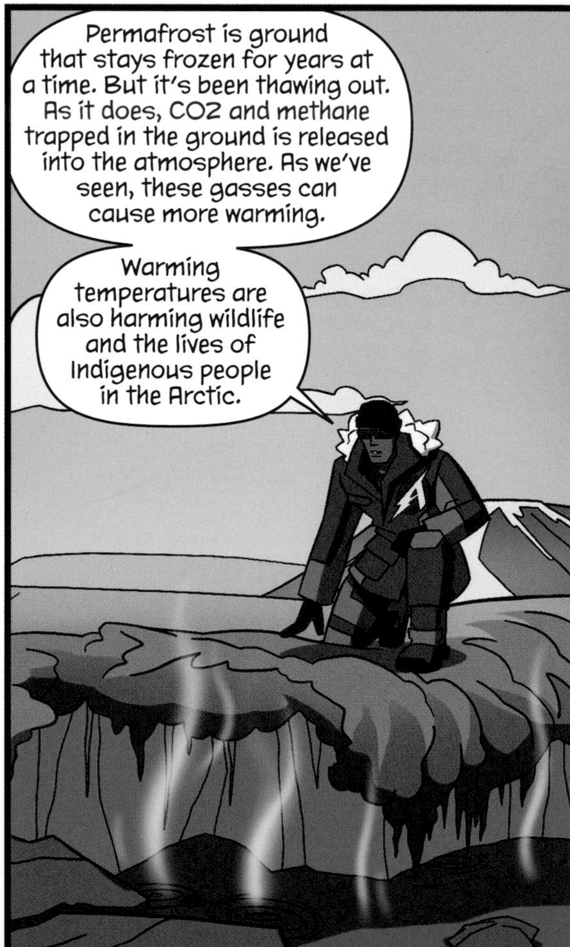
Permafrost is ground that stays frozen for years at a time. But it's been thawing out. As it does, CO2 and methane trapped in the ground is released into the atmosphere. As we've seen, these gasses can cause more warming.
Warming temperatures are also harming wildlife and the lives of Indigenous people in the Arctic.

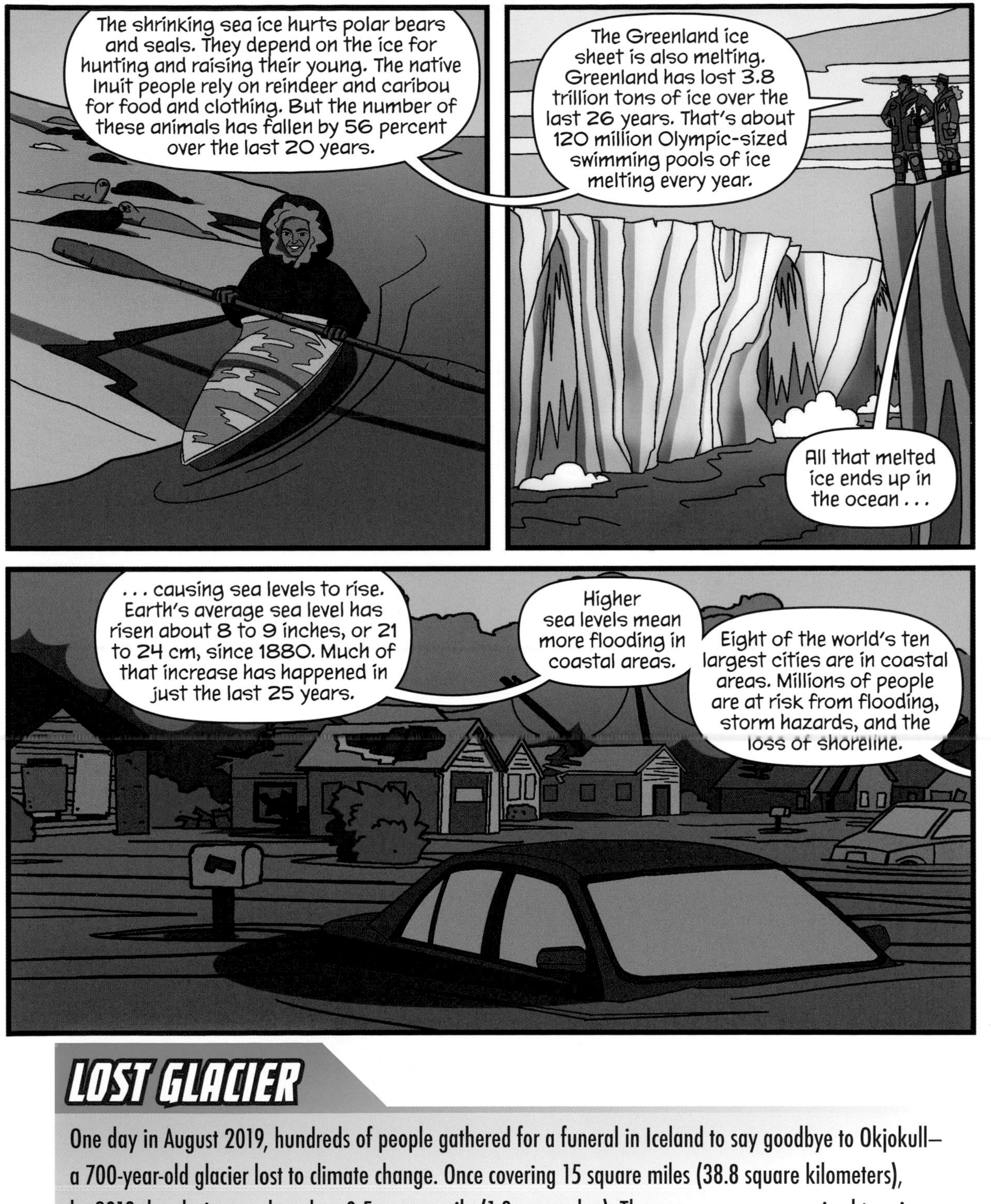
The shrinking sea ice hurts polar bears and seals. They depend on the ice for hunting and raising their young. The native Inuit people rely on reindeer and caribou for food and clothing. But the number of these animals has fallen by 56 percent over the last 20 years.
The Greenland ice sheet is also melting. Greenland has lost 3.8 trillion tons of ice over the last 26 years. That's about 120 million Olympic-sized swimming pools of ice melting every year.
All that melted ice ends up in the ocean . . .
. . . causing sea levels to rise. Earth's average sea level has risen about 8 to 9 inches, or 21 to 24 cm, since 1880. Much of that increase has happened in just the last 25 years.
Higher sea levels mean more flooding in coastal areas.
Eight of the world's ten largest cities are in coastal areas. Millions of people are at risk from flooding, storm hazards, and the loss of shoreline.

LOST GLACIER

One day in August 2019, hundreds of people gathered for a funeral in Iceland to say goodbye to Okjokull—a 700-year-old glacier lost to climate change. Once covering 15 square miles (38.8 square kilometers), by 2019 the glacier was less than 0.5 square mile (1.3 square km). The ceremony was organized to raise awareness about climate change. Iceland fears it could lose all of its glaciers by 2200.

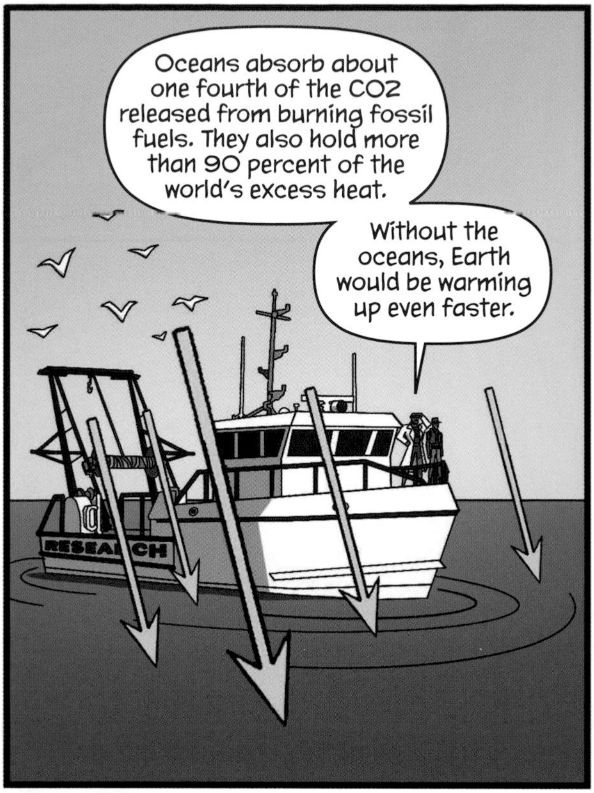
Oceans absorb about one fourth of the CO2 released from burning fossil fuels. They also hold more than 90 percent of the world's excess heat.
Without the oceans, Earth would be warming up even faster.

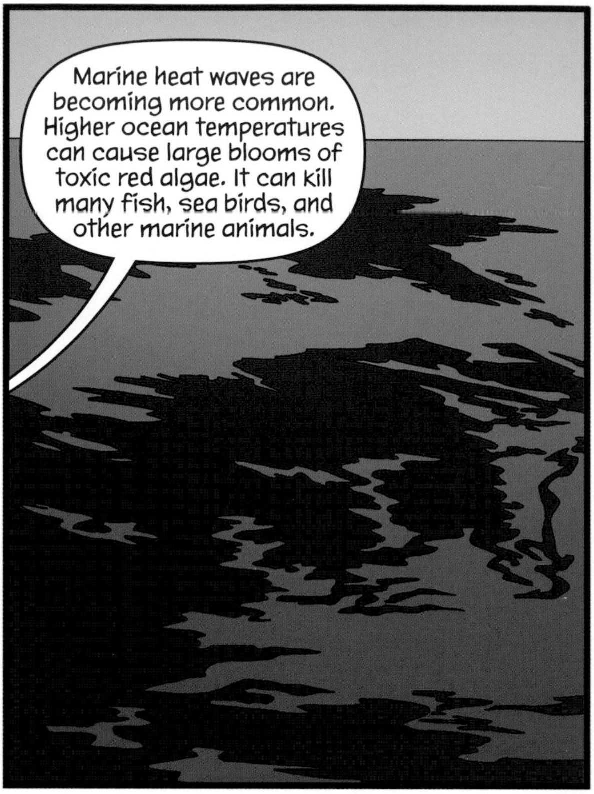
Marine heat waves are becoming more common. Higher ocean temperatures can cause large blooms of toxic red algae. It can kill many fish, sea birds, and other marine animals.

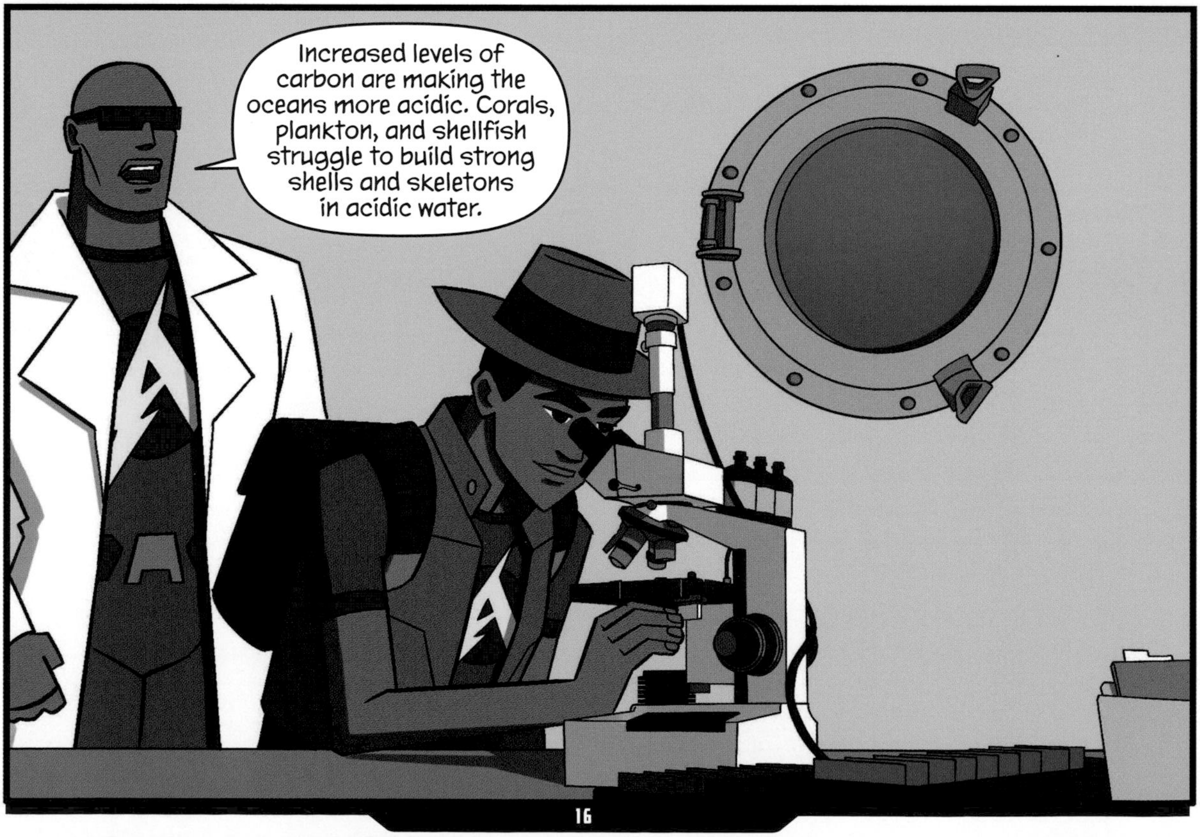
Increased levels of carbon are making the oceans more acidic. Corals, plankton, and shellfish struggle to build strong shells and skeletons in acidic water.

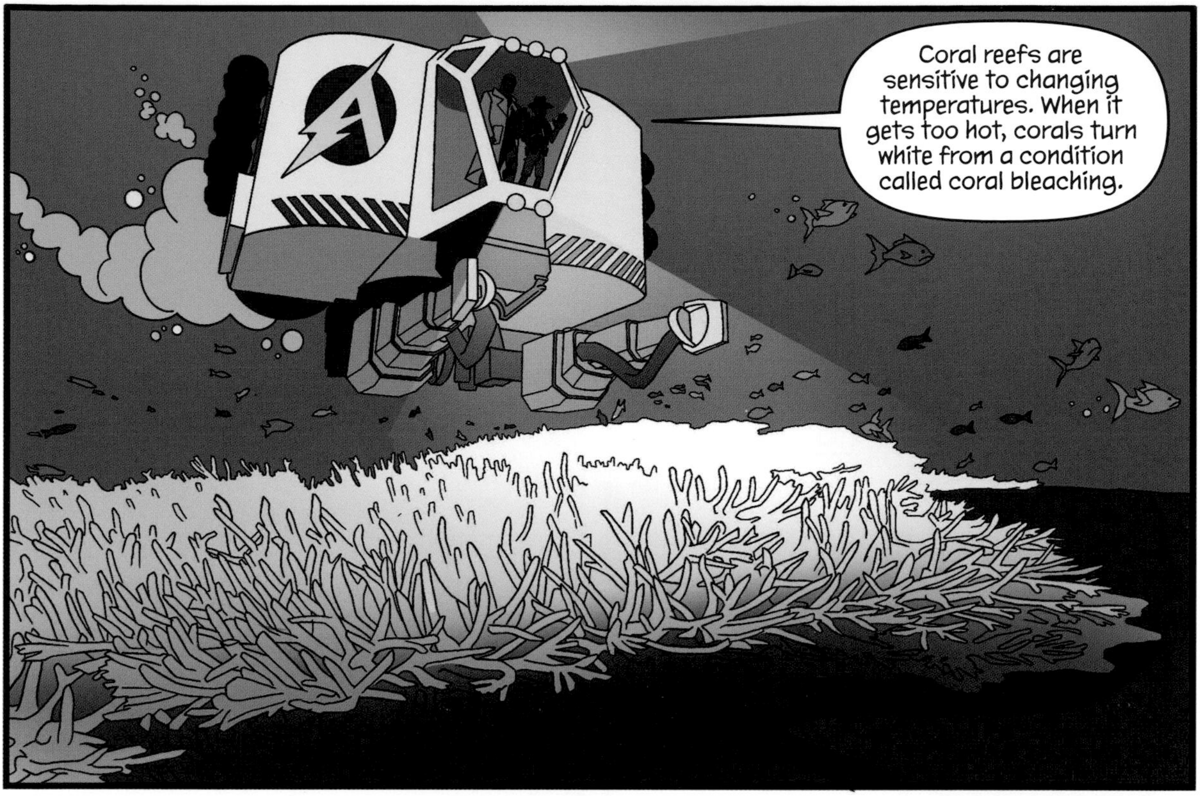
Coral reefs are sensitive to changing temperatures. When it gets too hot, corals turn white from a condition called coral bleaching.

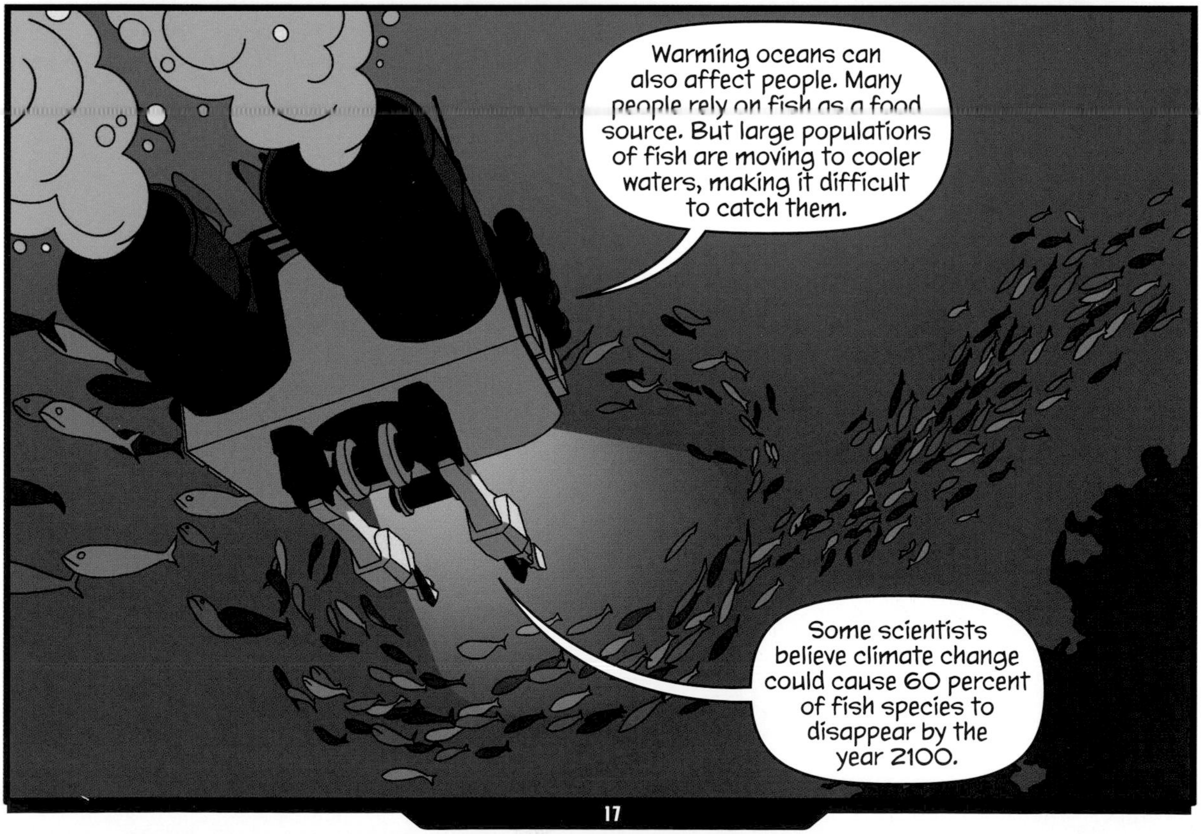
Warming oceans can also affect people. Many people rely on fish as a food source. But large populations of fish are moving to cooler waters, making it difficult to catch them.
Some scientists believe climate change could cause 60 percent of fish species to disappear by the year 2100.

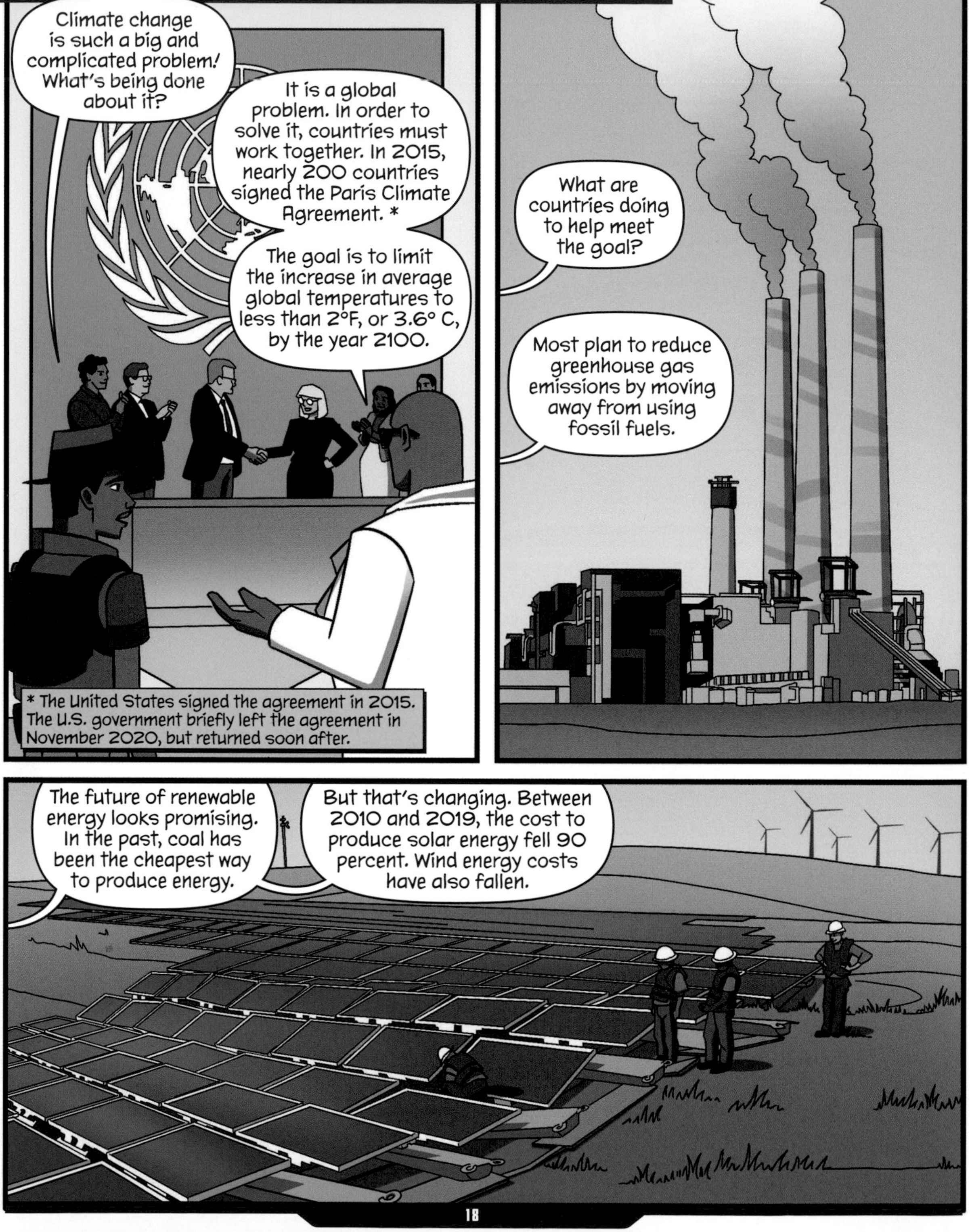
Climate change is such a big and complicated problem! What's being done about it?
It is a global problem. In order to solve it, countries must work together. In 2015, nearly 200 countries signed the Paris Climate Agreement. *
The goal is to limit the increase in average global temperatures to less than 2°F, or 3.6° C, by the year 2100.
* The United States signed the agreement in 2015. The U.S. government briefly left the agreement in November 2020, but returned soon after.
What are countries doing to help meet the goal?
Most plan to reduce greenhouse gas emissions by moving away from using fossil fuels.
The future of renewable energy looks promising. In the past, coal has been the cheapest way to produce energy.
But that's changing. Between 2010 and 2019, the cost to produce solar energy fell 90 percent. Wind energy costs have also fallen.

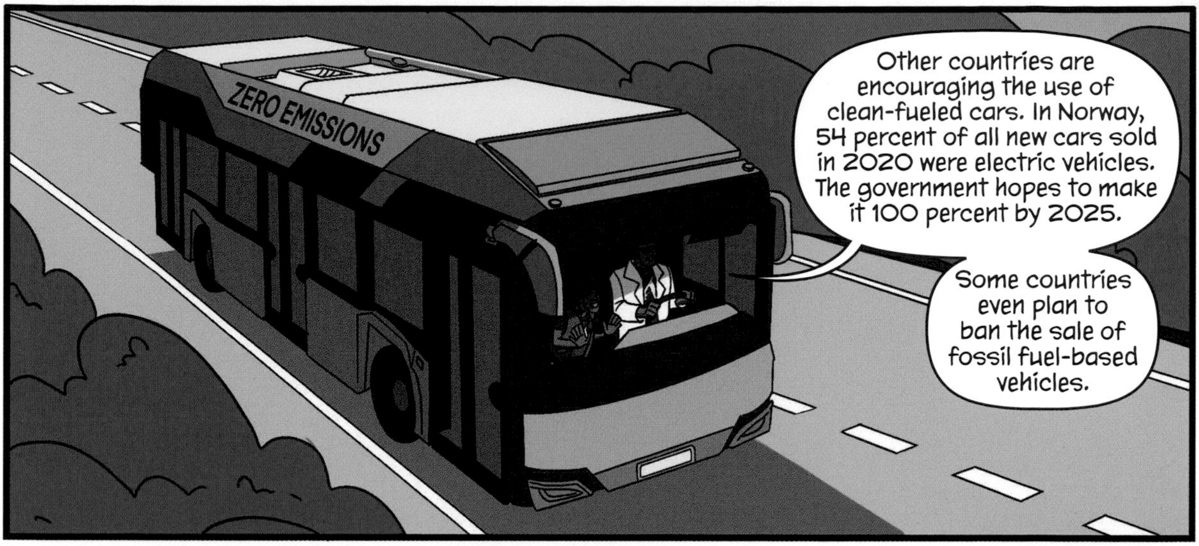
ZERO EMISSIONS
Other countries are encouraging the use of clean-fueled cars. In Norway, 54 percent of all new cars sold in 2020 were electric vehicles. The government hopes to make it 100 percent by 2025.
Some countries even plan to ban the sale of fossil fuel-based vehicles.

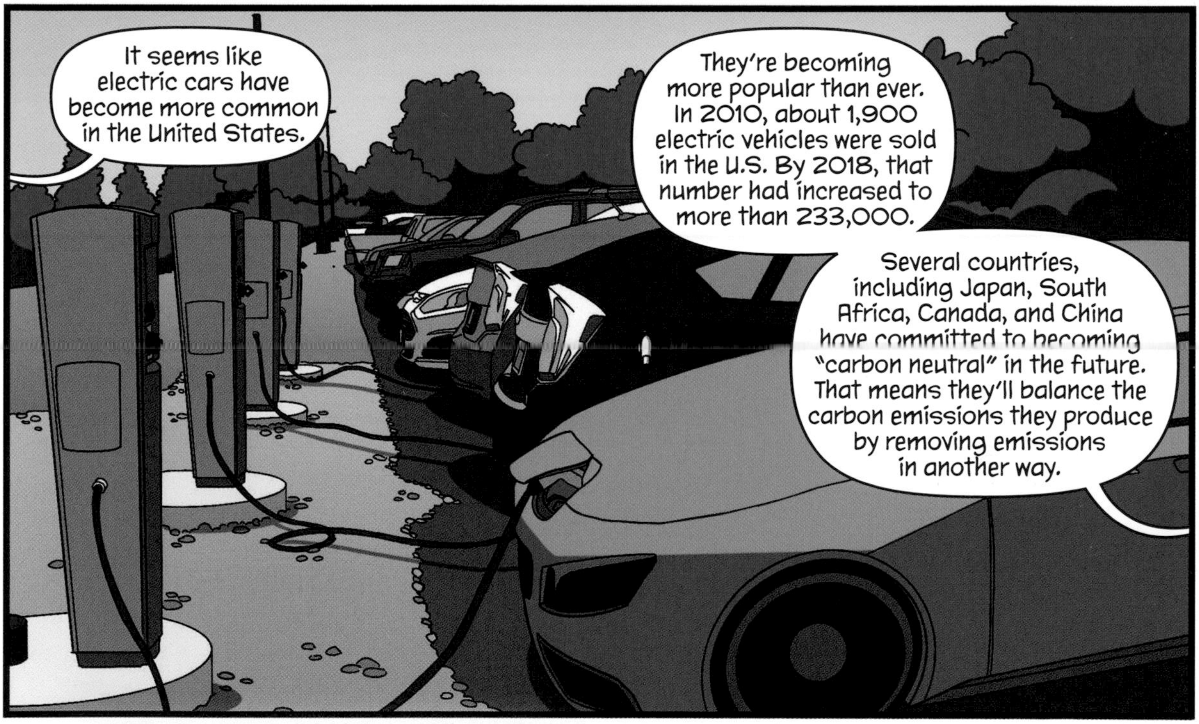
It seems like electric cars have become more common in the United States.
They're becoming more popular than ever. In 2010, about 1,900 electric vehicles were sold in the U.S. By 2018, that number had increased to more than 233,000.
Several countries, including Japan, South Africa, Canada, and China have committed to becoming "carbon neutral" in the future. That means they'll balance the carbon emissions they produce by removing emissions in another way.

CLIMATE WARNINGS

To remind drivers about how fossil fuels contribute to climate change, the city of Cambridge, Massachusetts has taken a new approach. The city requires all gas pumps to display bright yellow warning stickers. They read, "Burning gasoline, diesel, and ethanol has major consequences on human health and the environment, including contributing to climate change."

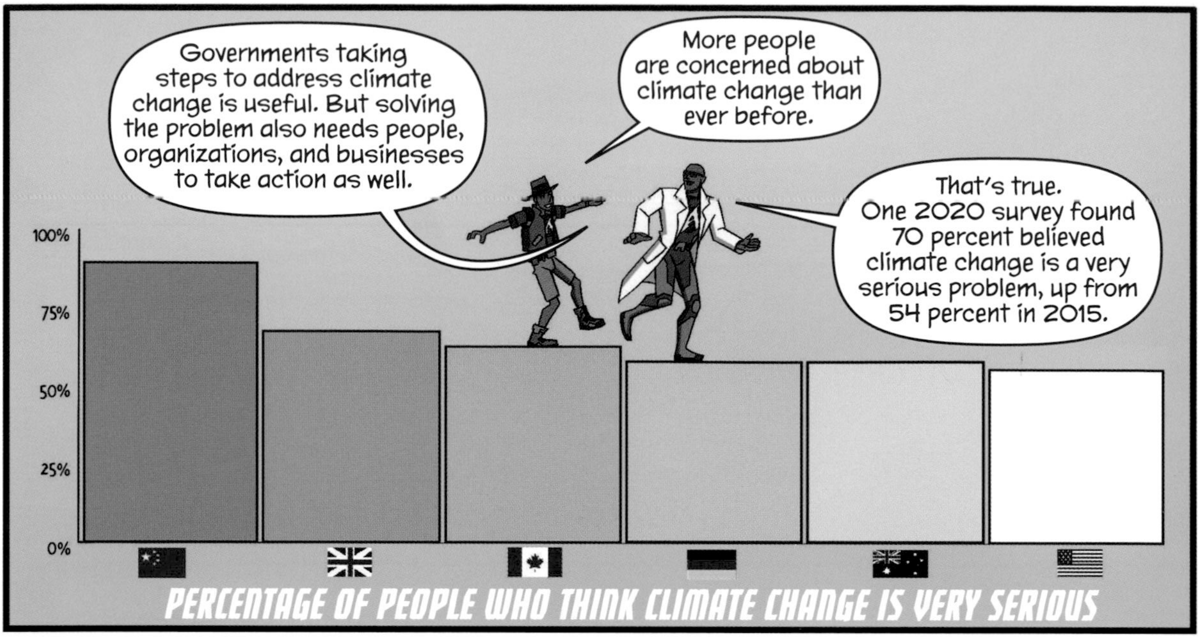
Governments taking steps to address climate change is useful. But solving the problem also needs people, organizations, and businesses to take action as well.
More people are concerned about climate change than ever before.
That's true. One 2020 survey found 70 percent believed climate change is a very serious problem, up from 54 percent in 2015.
100%
75%
50%
25%
0%
PERCENTAGE OF PEOPLE WHO THINK CLIMATE CHANGE IS VERY SERIOUS

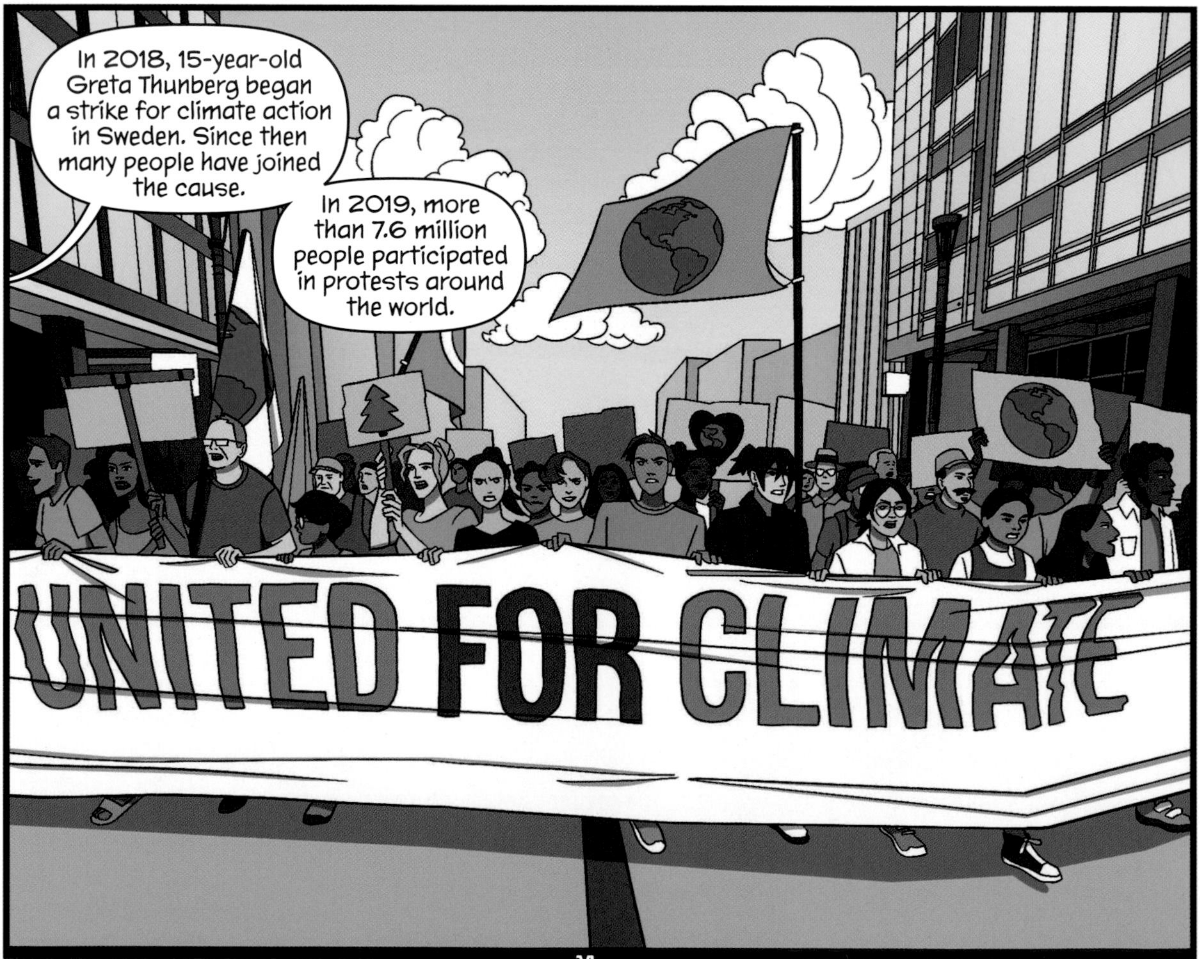
In 2018, 15-year-old Greta Thunberg began a strike for climate action in Sweden. Since then many people have joined the cause.
In 2019, more than 7.6 million people participated in protests around the world.
UNITED FOR CLIMATE

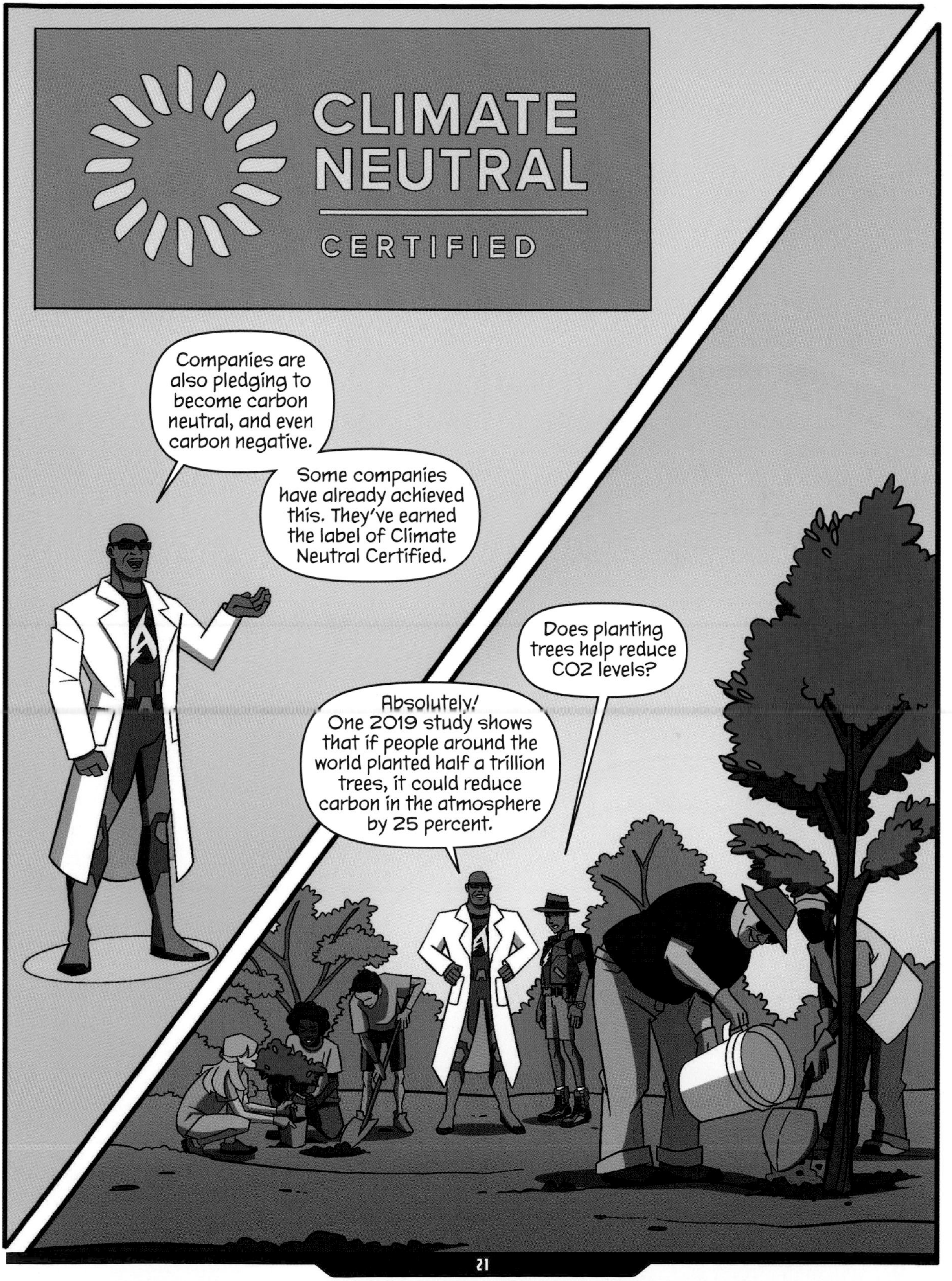
CLIMATE NEUTRAL
CERTIFIED
Companies are also pledging to become carbon neutral, and even carbon negative.
Some companies have already achieved this. They've earned the label of Climate Neutral Certified.
Does planting trees help reduce CO2 levels?
Absolutely! One 2019 study shows that if people around the world planted half a trillion trees, it could reduce carbon in the atmosphere by 25 percent.

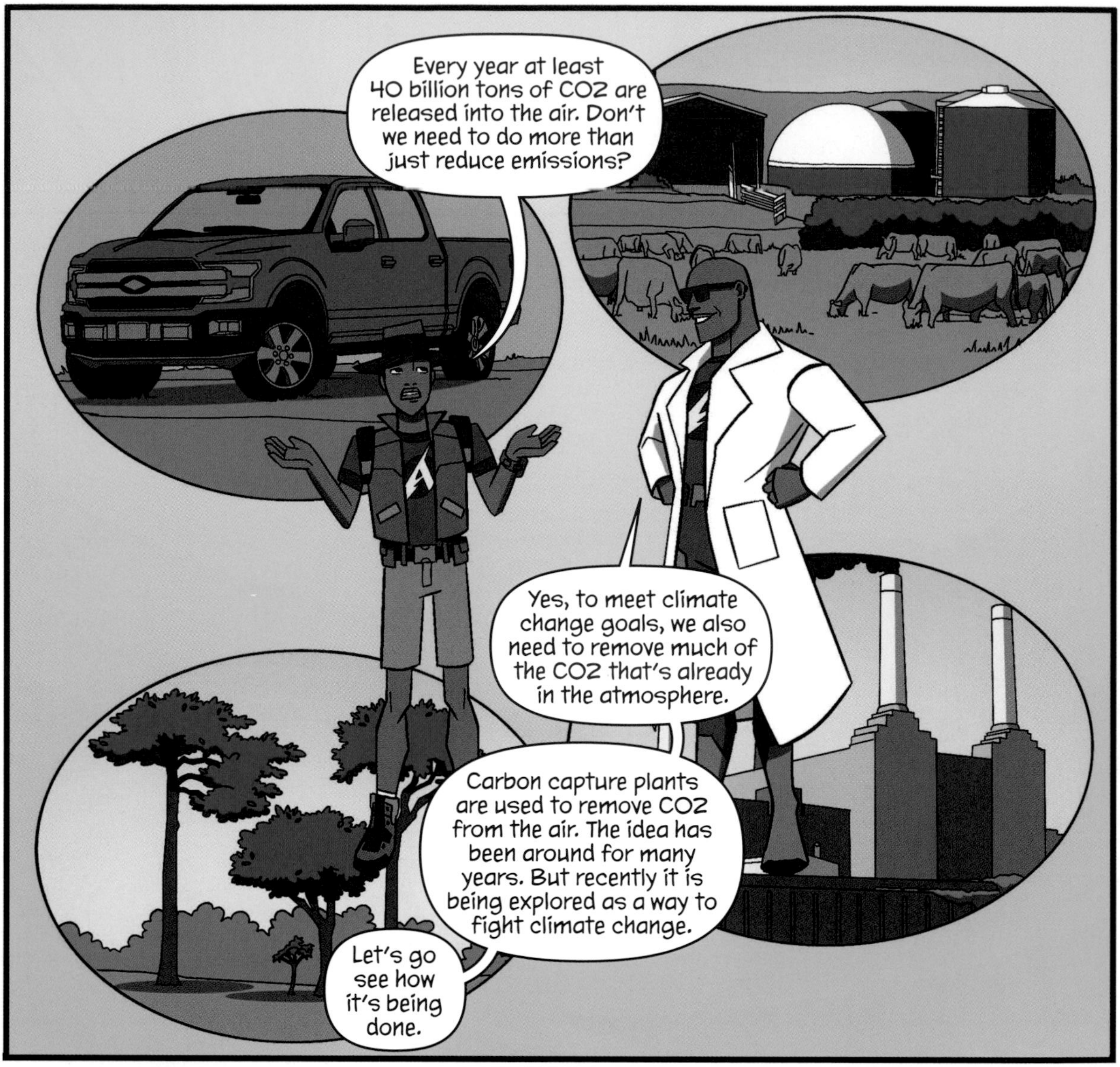
Every year at least 40 billion tons of CO2 are released into the air. Don't we need to do more than just reduce emissions?
Yes, to meet climate change goals, we also need to remove much of the CO2 that's already in the atmosphere.
Carbon capture plants are used to remove CO2 from the air. The idea has been around for many years. But recently it is being explored as a way to fight climate change.
Let's go see how it's being done.

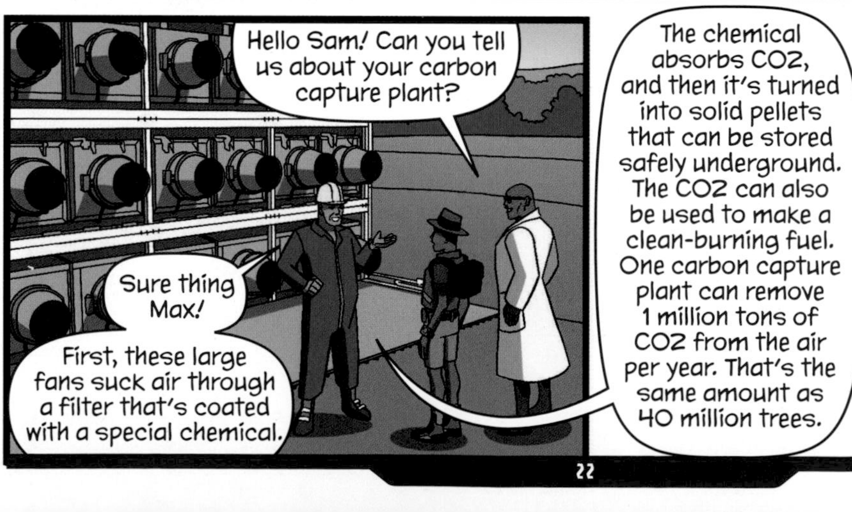
Hello Sam! Can you tell us about your carbon capture plant?
Sure thing Max!
First, these large fans suck air through a filter that's coated with a special chemical.
The chemical absorbs CO2, and then it's turned into solid pellets that can be stored safely underground. The CO2 can also be used to make a clean-burning fuel. One carbon capture plant can remove 1 million tons of CO2 from the air per year. That's the same amount as 40 million trees.

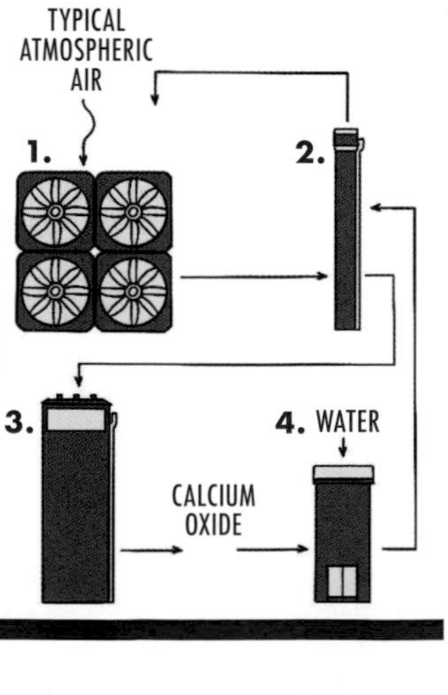
TYPICAL ATMOSPHERIC AIR
1.
2.
3.
4. WATER
CALCIUM OXIDE

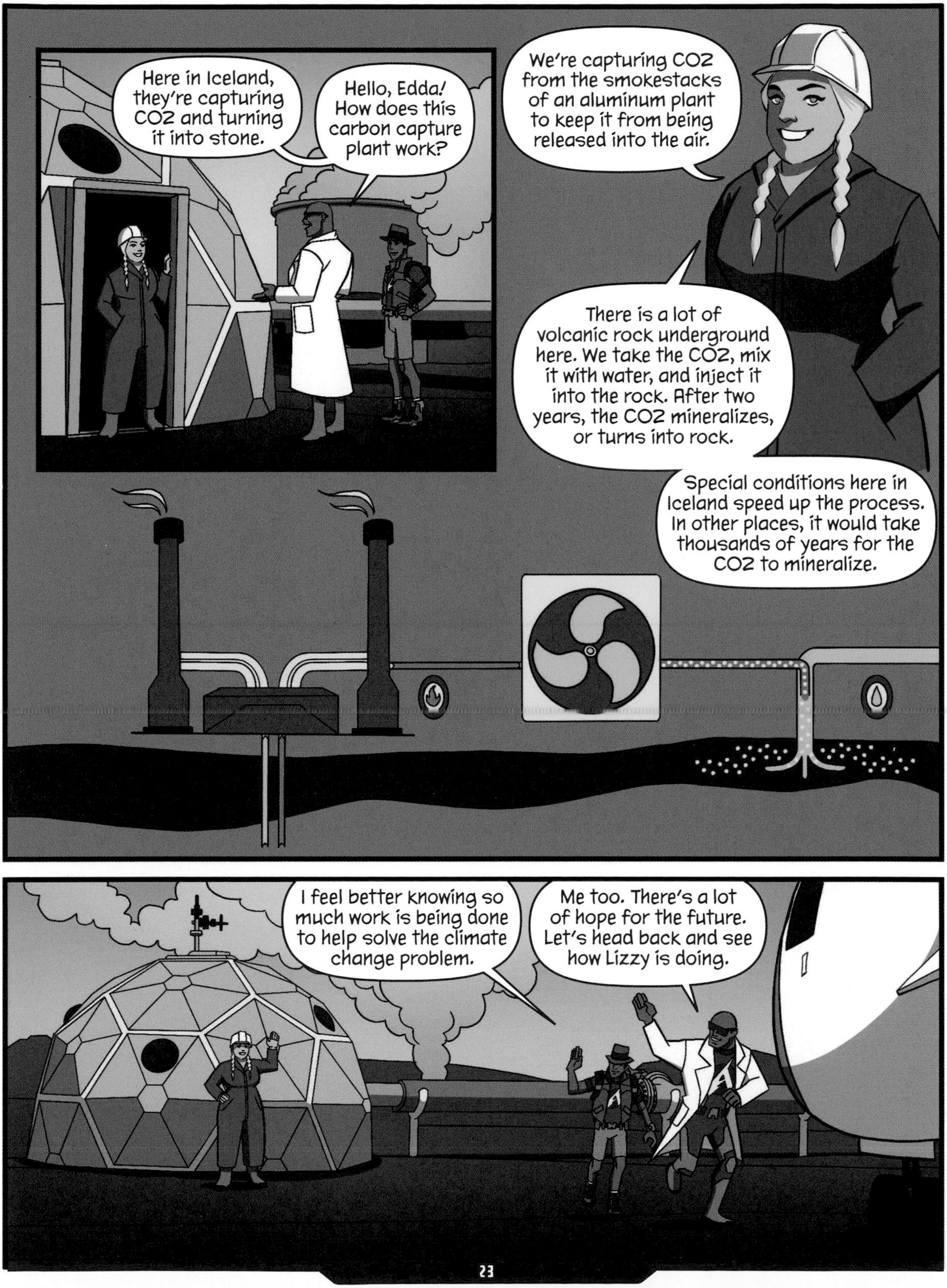
Here in Iceland, they're capturing CO2 and turning it into stone.
Hello, Edda! How does this carbon capture plant work?
We're capturing CO2 from the smokestacks of an aluminum plant to keep it from being released into the air.
There is a lot of volcanic rock underground here. We take the CO2, mix it with water, and inject it into the rock. After two years, the CO2 mineralizes, or turns into rock.
Special conditions here in Iceland speed up the process. In other places, it would take thousands of years for the CO2 to mineralize.
I feel better knowing so much work is being done to help solve the climate change problem.
Me too. There's a lot of hope for the future. Let's head back and see how Lizzy is doing.

SECTION 4: *TAKING ACTION*

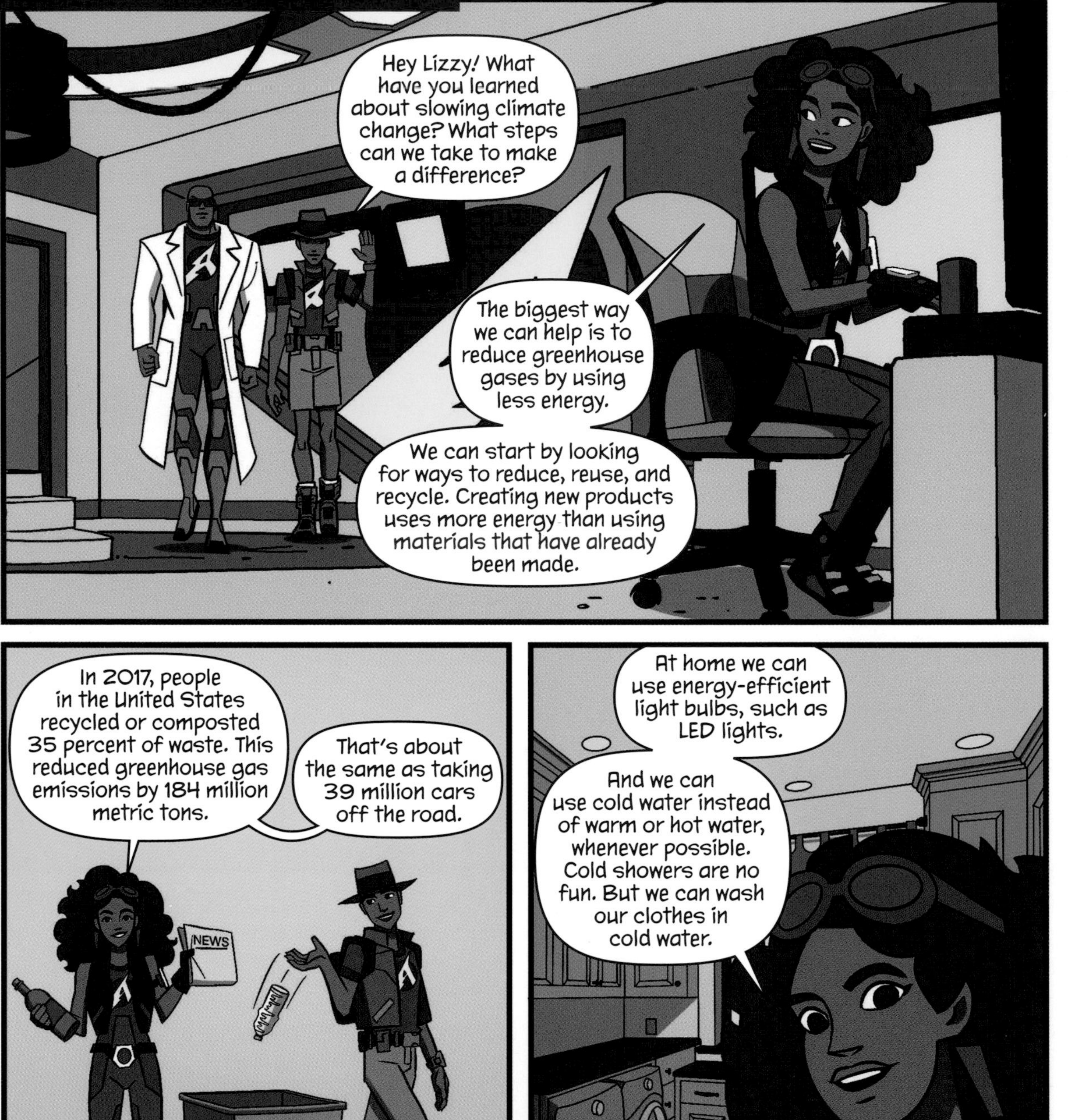

Hey Lizzy! What have you learned about slowing climate change? What steps can we take to make a difference?
The biggest way we can help is to reduce greenhouse gases by using less energy.
We can start by looking for ways to reduce, reuse, and recycle. Creating new products uses more energy than using materials that have already been made.
In 2017, people in the United States recycled or composted 35 percent of waste. This reduced greenhouse gas emissions by 184 million metric tons.
That's about the same as taking 39 million cars off the road.
NEWS
At home we can use energy-efficient light bulbs, such as LED lights.
And we can use cold water instead of warm or hot water, whenever possible. Cold showers are no fun. But we can wash our clothes in cold water.

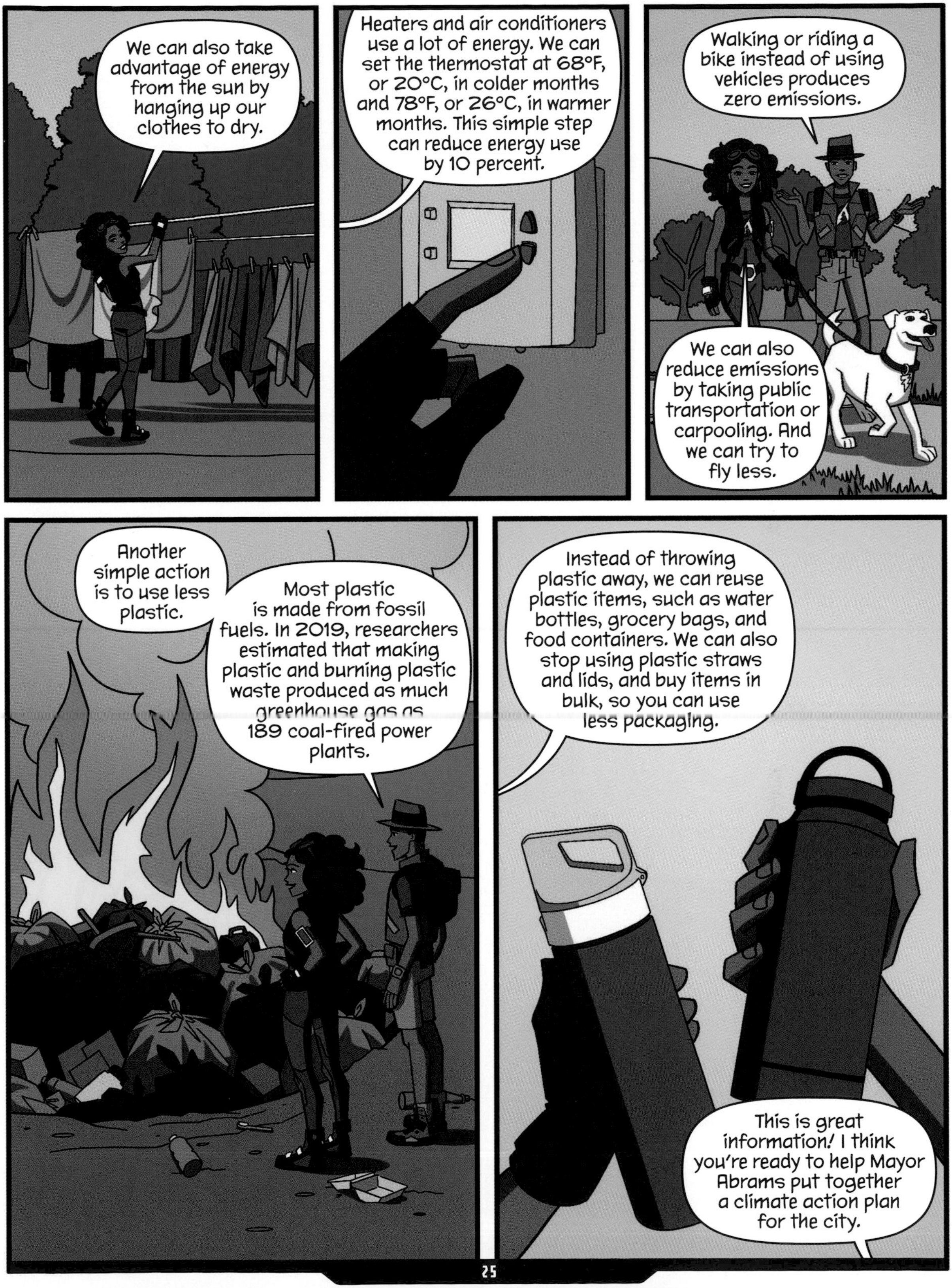
We can also take advantage of energy from the sun by hanging up our clothes to dry.
Heaters and air conditioners use a lot of energy. We can set the thermostat at 68°F, or 20°C, in colder months and 78°F, or 26°C, in warmer months. This simple step can reduce energy use by 10 percent.
Walking or riding a bike instead of using vehicles produces zero emissions.
We can also reduce emissions by taking public transportation or carpooling. And we can try to fly less.
Another simple action is to use less plastic.
Most plastic is made from fossil fuels. In 2019, researchers estimated that making plastic and burning plastic waste produced as much greenhouse gas as 189 coal-fired power plants.
Instead of throwing plastic away, we can reuse plastic items, such as water bottles, grocery bags, and food containers. We can also stop using plastic straws and lids, and buy items in bulk, so you can use less packaging.
This is great information! I think you're ready to help Mayor Abrams put together a climate action plan for the city.

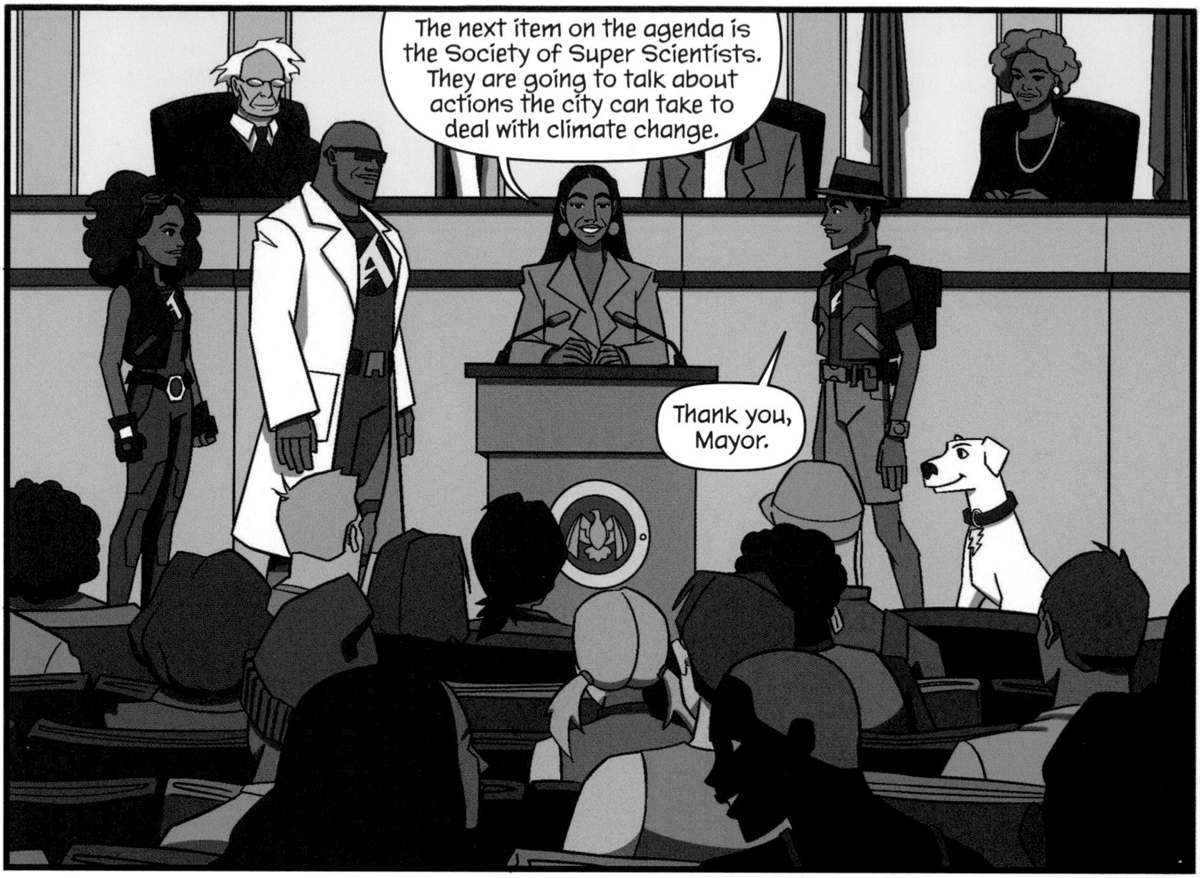
The next item on the agenda is the Society of Super Scientists. They are going to talk about actions the city can take to deal with climate change.
Thank you, Mayor.

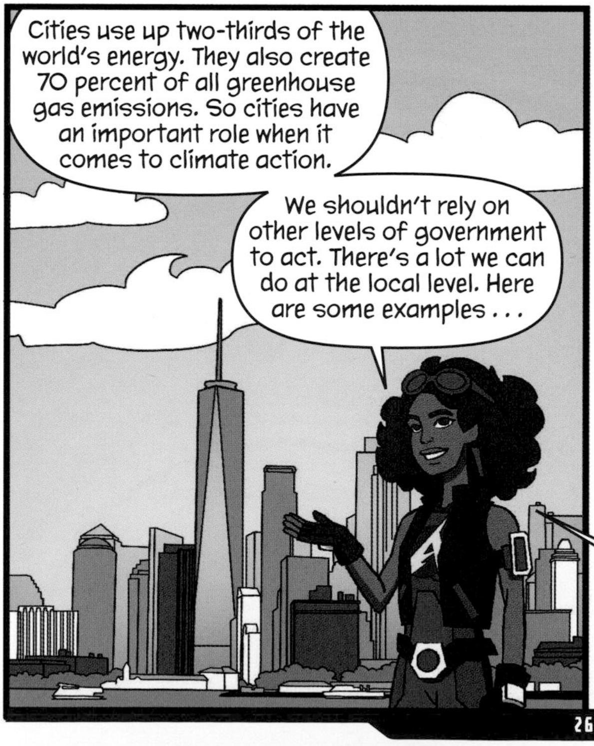
Cities use up two-thirds of the world's energy. They also create 70 percent of all greenhouse gas emissions. So cities have an important role when it comes to climate action.
We shouldn't rely on other levels of government to act. There's a lot we can do at the local level. Here are some examples . . .

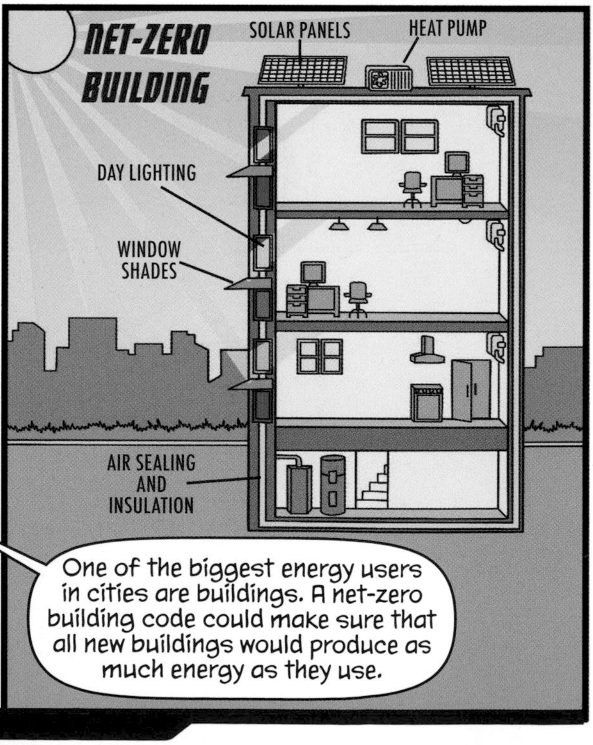
NET-ZERO BUILDING
SOLAR PANELS
HEAT PUMP
DAY LIGHTING
WINDOW SHADES
AIR SEALING AND INSULATION
One of the biggest energy users in cities are buildings. A net-zero building code could make sure that all new buildings would produce as much energy as they use.

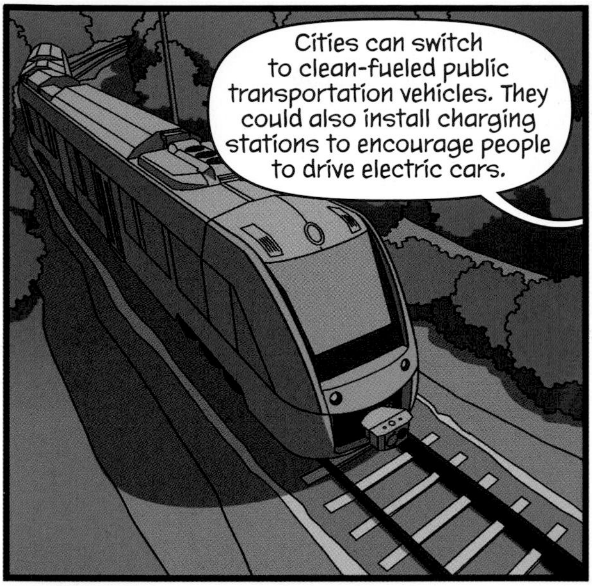
Cities can switch to clean-fueled public transportation vehicles. They could also install charging stations to encourage people to drive electric cars.

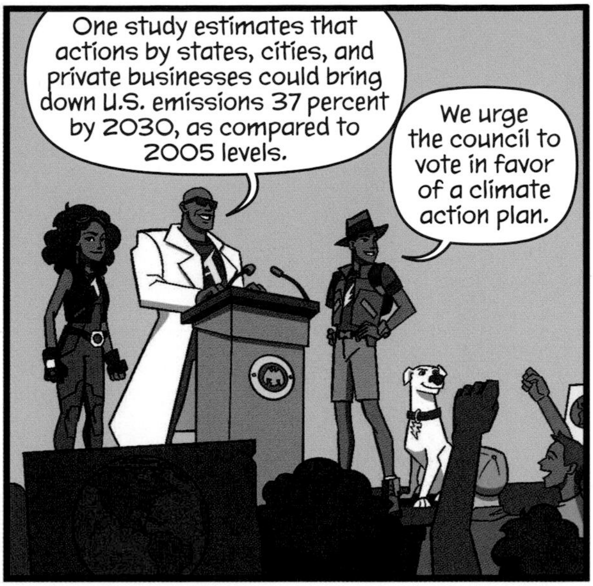
One study estimates that actions by states, cities, and private businesses could bring down U.S. emissions 37 percent by 2030, as compared to 2005 levels.
We urge the council to vote in favor of a climate action plan.

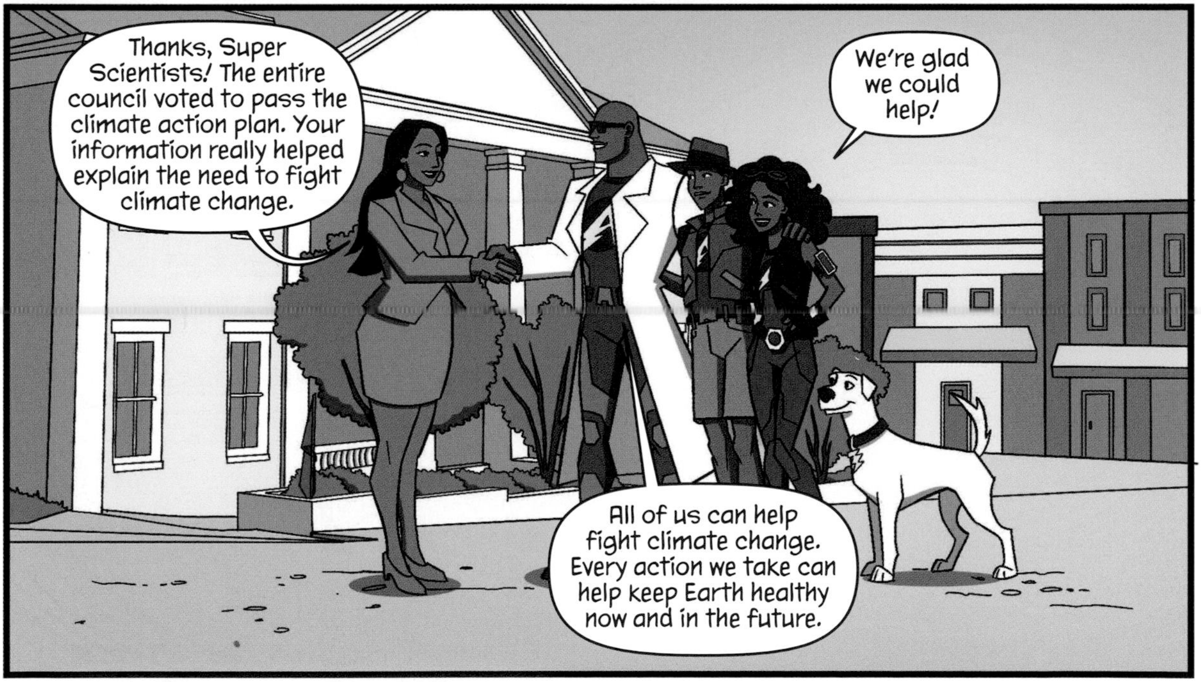
Thanks, Super Scientists! The entire council voted to pass the climate action plan. Your information really helped explain the need to fight climate change.
We're glad we could help!
All of us can help fight climate change. Every action we take can help keep Earth healthy now and in the future.

SEA TURTLE CRISIS

Scientists have discovered global warming is affecting the gender of sea turtles. When sand temperatures of turtle nests are warmer, it results in more females. Scientists found that 99 percent of hatchlings from one nesting site in Australia were female. Similar trends have been discovered in other nesting grounds. Experts have serious concerns about the future of sea turtle populations.

HOPE FOR THE CLIMATE

Climate change might seem like an overwhelming and grim problem. But there are many bright spots that provide rays of hope for the future.

General Motors (GM) is one of the world's largest automakers. The company announced that it would make and sell only electric cars by 2035. The company's leader also promised GM would be net carbon neutral by 2040.

In September 2020, California banned the sale of all new gasoline-powered vehicles by 2035. The state was soon followed by New Jersey and Massachusetts. They adopted similar bans, also with targets of 2035.

Several large technology companies have begun adopting bold plans to use 100 percent renewable energy. They plan to become carbon neutral, or even carbon negative, within the next 10 to 15 years.

Senator Sheldon Whitehouse first gave a speech urging action on climate change in April 2012. He continued giving the same speech every week for the next nine years. He finally ended his run with his 279th speech, after climate change measures began to be adopted in January 2021.

The country of Bhutan is carbon negative. It's the only country in the world that has achieved this milestone. Bhutan is a tiny country. It's about the size of Maryland, and 70 percent of its land is covered by trees. It is powered completely by hydropower, much of which they export to other countries.

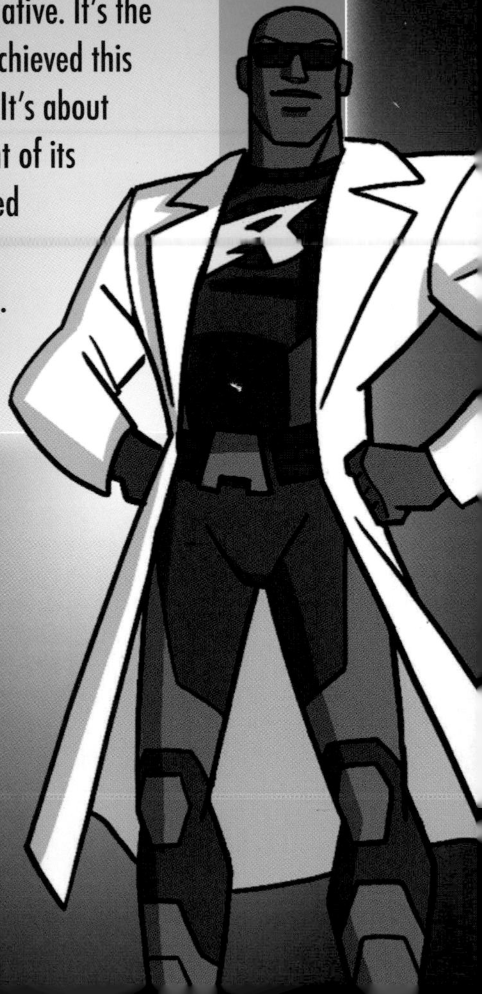

GLOSSARY

albedo effect (al-BEE-do ih-FEKT)—the ability of light surfaces to reflect more solar energy than dark surfaces

atmosphere (AT-muh-sfeer)—the mixture of gases that surrounds a planet

climate (KLY-muht)—the average weather of a place over a long period of time

compost (KAHM-pohst)—recycling organic material, such as leaves and food scraps, to allow it to break down into fertilizer

drought (drout)—a long period without rain

emissions (ee-MIH-shunz)—substances discharged into the air

fossil fuel (FAH-suhl FYOOL)—a fuel formed in the Earth from the remains of plants and animals; coal, oil, and natural gas are fossil fuels

greenhouse gas (GREEN-hows GAS)—a gas, such as carbon dioxide or methane, in Earth's atmosphere that traps heat energy from the sun

permafrost (PUR-muh-frawst)—a layer of ground that stays frozen

renewable energy (ri-NOO-uh-buhl EN-ur-jee)—power from sources that can never be used up, such as wind, water, and the Sun

READ MORE

DK. *Findout! Climate Change.* New York: DK Publishing, 2020.

Herman, Gail. *What is Climate Change?* New York: Penguin Random House, 2018.

Minoglio, Andrea. *Our World Out of Balance: Understanding Climate Change and What We Can Do.* San Francisco: Blue Dot Kids Press, 2021.

INTERNET SITES

American Museum of Natural History: Climate Change
amnh.org/explore/ology/climate-change

Climate Basics for Kids
c2es.org/content/climate-basics-for-kids

Kids Against Climate Change
kidsagainstclimatechange.co

NASA: Climate Kids
climatekids.nasa.gov/climate-change-meaning

INDEX

ABOUT THE AUTHOR

Carol Kim is the author of several fiction and nonfiction books for kids. She enjoys researching and uncovering little-known facts and sharing what she learns with young readers. Carol lives in Austin, Texas, with her family. Learn more about her and her latest books at her website, CarolKimBooks.com.